POLITICAL V

By the same author

IN THE NAME OF SCIENCE
NUCLEAR SECRECY AND FOREIGN POLICY

POLITICAL VIOLENCE

The
Behavioral Process

H. L. NIEBURG

ST. MARTIN'S PRESS, NEW YORK

Fourth Printing 1970

Library of Congress catalog card number: *78-83408*

The author wishes to thank Random House, Inc. for
permission to use W. H. Auden's poem, "Law Like Love",
from *The Collected Poetry of W. H. Auden.*
Copyright © 1945 by Random House, Inc.

Cover photograph courtesy of WIDE WORLD PHOTOS

Designed by Sally Shaw

Manufactured in the United States of America

St. Martin's Press, 175 Fifth Ave., New York 10010

PREFACE

This book is based upon work done originally for the National Commission on the Causes and Prevention of Violence established by the President following the assassination of Robert F. Kennedy. My assignment was of a general and theoretical nature, to formulate an analytical matrix relating extreme forms of social action, including assassination, to the whole continuum of political behavior. It was hoped that my contribution might be of some diagnostic value to the commission in the task of integrating a wide variety of highly specialized and clinical findings of psychiatrists, criminologists, Secret Service officials, and others concerned with extreme behavior.

The original monograph, written under pressure of a deadline, was entitled "Assassination and the Continuum of Political Behavior." I do not know what value it had for the commission, but it had great value to me. As a consequence of this sudden immersion in the subject of political violence (an interest I have pursued since 1962), I found myself full of data and ideas and an urge to communicate. Over a period of several months, I completely revised and expanded the original monograph into this present work. Much of the specific data on political assassination in the original paper has been discarded in favor of an attempt to create a compelling model of the role played by all degrees and kinds of political violence in the social process.

I am indebted to William Crotty, who as co-director of the Task Force on Political Assassination gave me the original assignment. I wish to thank Irving Louis Horowitz and Daniel Glaser for their helpful suggestions on the first draft of this book, and the Rockefeller Foundation for its support, especially Kenneth Thompson, Vice President. I am grateful to a number of students at the University of Wisconsin, Milwaukee, especially Harvey Silverstein, Tom Rose, and James Bingen, whose questions and comments deepened our mutual probing of the subject, and who aided my research; and to my daughter, Elizabeth, who worked on the index and references.

This book and many other things would have been quite impossible without the skill and devotion of my wife, who not only deciphered my notes but, more important, translated my mind and preserved my body and soul. To my wife, Janet, then, with love and gladness.

H. L. Nieburg

Mequon, Wisconsin
January 1969

CONTENTS

POLITICAL VIOLENCE

There is nothing so eagerly believed as the things that are not so.

Darrow, 1932, p. 319

THE RELEVANCE OF VIOLENCE

1

The present generation is learning anew a lesson which many generations have learned in the past, sometimes too late: there are in human affairs great natural forces, comparable in their power to destroy to hurricanes or earthquakes. Highly organized societies, for all their power and magnificence, are delicately balanced organisms. All the inherent powers of human relations are brought together in a volatile fusion. Social cohesion does not come about automatically and cannot be taken for granted; it requires continuous attention and concern.

New images have burst upon the scene: "long hot summers," confrontation politics in street and campus, an armaments race between suburb and ghetto. The symbols and paraphernalia of internal warfare crash against the citadels of American complacency. Black militancy, student protest, frontlash and backlash in all varieties compete with each other for attention, adopting ever more shocking and violent tactics to prod and incite us. At the height of its glory, this most bountiful and generous society reels in confusion. Where is the American Dream? What is happening to the American miracle?

All our fondest theories of economic development and political stability totter and collapse in the face of riots, guerrilla warfare, assassinations. Events of this century have done much to shatter our self-confidence. Yet an attitude of despair is just as unhelpful as is our traditional self-righteous optimism. The best response to our present dilemmas is to recognize both the problems of our society and the still formidable resilience of our people and our institutions. The wrong attitude can generate a self-fulfilling prophecy. The disorders that threaten us are far from apocalyptic. But they cannot be dismissed or merely disapproved, and certainly they should not be ignored.

In the context of the social system in which it occurs, a widespread appeal to violence in a sense represents a strain toward social reintegration and legitimacy. We need to know not only how and why the social barriers against extremism are breached, but also how society can constructively assimilate demands for change. Ugly acts break forth at the perimeters of even the most stable social systems. Many social institutions, government and politics, the family and the church, must localize, contain, repress, and redirect such isolated threats. It is not merely the presence of violence that constitutes a problem. Our society is challenged by the kind of violence, its effects in inhibiting creative political leadership, which threatens the imminent deadlock of escalated and counterescalated force, the general loss of regard for our customary social institutions, and the spread of violence throughout the social system. Even the loss of a popular leader to a lone assassin's bullet is not the problem; rather, the problem is the existence of conditions that divide our society, which may make violence a pattern and which may undermine the recuperative powers of the society.

The problem of political violence raises virtually every other major issue in political sociology and political theory as well as every major unresolved issue of public policy and the social system. We are faced with a whole series of national problems, said a despairing George F. Kennan at Princeton, "each of which, if not soon met in some adequate manner, has the capability of bringing most grievous, perhaps mortal, damage to our national life. Yet to none of which has our response as a nation been to date in any way adequate" *(New York Times,* December 4, 1968, p. 62).

The Problem of Perspective

Extreme and violent political behavior cannot be dismissed as erratic, exceptional, and meaningless. To set it apart from the processes that are characteristic of society is to ignore the continuum that exists between peaceable and disruptive behavior; it is to deny the role of violence in creating and testing political legitimacy and in conditioning the terms of all social bargaining and adjustment. Violence in all its forms, up to and including assassination, is a natural form of political behavior. The conceptual framework of this study, unlike most that have appeared before, views disorder as intrinsically related to the social process.

For generations the prevalence of social violence, however obvious, has been overlooked, repressed, or misconstrued. Until recently, the social sciences have conspicuously omitted to recognize or study seriously the political dynamics and dimensions of violent behavior except to treat it as aberrant and atypical, involving only backward nations and demented individuals. The prevalence of violent incidents marking virtually every turning place of our history, both domestic and international, has been ascribed to evil ideologies, unenlightened political systems, and power-hungry, violent men. The social sciences have clung to a blind tranquillity that has not fostered understanding of the power of events to shatter or dismay.

Polarization and confrontation in American society have been long in coming and have deep roots. The violence of the desperate and the poor could be neglected when it was directed inward and did not jeopardize our relative calm. The invasion of our immediate environment by the reality of confrontation and violence awakens us. However, once more there is no guarantee that we can interpret our troubles without self-justifying blinders.

A sense of optimism came in the year 1968; the ghettos of major cities remained relatively quiet. By then the riots had spread to smaller industrial towns and university campuses. The clashes with police of the Chicago convention involved primarily white middle-class youth; the blacks on Chicago's South Side kept the lid on and watched bemused. But optimism may be unwarranted. In fact, it may be hazardous. It may tend again to foster complacency at a time when black communities are organizing for guerrilla warfare, which in the next crunch may prove far more deadly and destructive.

We find it difficult to admit that the threat of violence—pure pain and damage—can be used to coerce and to deter, to intimidate and to blackmail, to demoralize and to paralyze, purposefully and meaningfully in a process of social bargaining. Since World War II, we have come to understand violence as a dimension of international politics, but until the riots and rebellions of the 1960s we have been loath to apply the same intelligence to domestic affairs. This failure in itself has contributed to the current crisis by insulating the status quo against timely and responsive change, abetting the buildup of social deficits and unsatisfied demands. Just as the legalistic pacifism of the world's democracies contributed to the massive violence of two world wars, so our unwillingness to look domestic violence in the face may again lead us to formulas of unconditional surrender and "final solutions" in the name of perpetual peace.

Such a reaction is manifest in the search for "law and order," which in its most popular version is a wish to return to the past. Ignoring normal dynamics of political violence has led us to a state of trauma and alarm, which is neither justified by the danger nor helpful in averting it. The public by a large majority endorses the gunning down of adolescent looters on the street; it blames agitators, communists, criminals, and even those who engage in positive efforts to treat the roots of social distress—anything but itself. "Law and order" becomes a slogan for repressing extremism by escalating the conflict rather than for attacking its causes.

The same failure of intelligence is evident in our interpretation of the tragic series of assassinations we have so lately endured. Virtually everything written on assassination dwells upon the tortured mind of the assassin, as though his tragic act were fully explainable by the accidents which created a flawed human being and gave him the chance in time and place and the weapons to act out an automatic, predestined, and therefore meaningless murder. This view may be reassuring, but it is false and misleading. It defeats common sense and understanding, and in the present crisis of our society it can lead us dangerously to take the wrong course.

To say that the role of the assassin has been overemphasized or misinterpreted is not, however, to propose that we neglect individual motivation and behavior, the basic units of the network of relationships that constitute a social system. Individuals are the concrete and dynamic monads of any larger abstraction. Private "motive" becomes a social fact when "it is made overt by the people of the society concerned, and when their regard for it affects the actions they perform after a homicide. Studying homicide in terms of 'motive' is often only a shorthand for studying social situations in which homicide occurs" (Bohannan, 1960, p. 252). One must look to dynamic social factors rather than isolated individual motives.

Murder, whether personal or political, is, like suicide, always a present possibility which society must expect and anticipate with mechanisms of defense, localization, and prevention. Isolated or recurrent acts of political extremism, like assassination, must be analyzed within the context of functional behavior. The definition of "deviance" always reflects normative values and is an extension of normative behavior which, at some level, is functional both for the deviant and for society. Overemphasis on individual causes takes a piece from the mosaic of our troubled times, thereby obscuring the general, social view that is necessary to a fuller understanding. In interpreting murder by postulating a unique individual pathology,we attempt to keep old values and institutions intact. Yet these values and institutions may themselves be the cause of individual acts of violence.

Like many forms of extreme behavior, violent acts may be looked upon as society's early warning system, revealing deep-rooted political conflicts which are gathering strength beneath the surface of social relations. In a real sense, the unbalanced individual is a sensitive telltale. The Middle Ages prized and honored the "village idiot"; Shakespeare put his most cogent truths in the mouths of jesters and knaves. The marginal individual suffers from the social strains and cleavages that run through his very life, unlike the "well-balanced" man who is protected by habit and social constraints and who is much slower to feel and to speak. Distraught and disturbed persons act and react without waiting for a new consensus. In this manner, they are both the victims and the heralds of social change.

Political extremism, whether for or against the status quo, is an indication that pressure is building against the chain of social relationships. The weakest links are the first to break and may, as has happened often in the past, precipitate larger crises. The assassination of Chicago car dealers (the Foreman brothers) by a Negro (who had bought a car he could not afford) foreshadowed the smashing of loan offices and automobile dealerships that erupted soon thereafter in Chicago and other cities. Many individuals in crisis signal a society in crisis. Whether violent action is deliberately contrived by those who wish to create a crisis situation or haplessly enacted by distressed individuals out of their own frenzy, the result is much the same. It is a commonplace that war and revolution are great catalysts of social change. Other forms of extreme behavior may have similar causes and effects.

Major social crises and dislocations by definition have major social causes. They are not the result of isolated conspiracies and plots, and they cannot be alleviated by efforts to stamp out all present and future conspiracies and plots. Social fits and seizures can be viewed as a form of "search behavior," a pragmatic trial-and-error method leading toward new political and social norms that better satisfy the strain toward security, predictability, and low-risk methods of conflict resolution which organized groups require and crave. Thus it is not enough to explain extremism by pointing to conditions which justify it. Rather, one must study patterns of behavior and the process by which they move from testing to selection and reinforcement.

Conflicts resolved by violence coexist with those resolved peacefully. Because conflict is not something to be eradicated, both values and the environmental sources of conflict must be considered in terms of the adequacy of the institutions of society to regulate conflict. Society and individuals should be equipped to deal with conflict and to profit from it. It should be as useful as it is inevitable.

A society without conflict is just as impossible as one without institutionalized ways of adjusting and regulating conflict.

In an important way, both violence and politics are outside the formal and legal processes of conflict resolution. Both represent the dynamic factors by which social consensus is itself reinforced and modified. Turbulence and disorder mark the frontier of history, where present and past break and blend into future, where vigor and growth are qualities which ultimately must redeem the inconvenience and unrest of an emerging social order.

It is self-defeating to study violence as if it were obscene, nor does recognition of its relevance condone or encourage it. Quite the contrary is true. Like many things, violence is deeply ambiguous in all its aspects, containing both functional and dysfunctional tendencies, capable of both positive and negative outcomes. In the view of the actor, all violence is reaction, that is, self-defense, flight, the desire to fight one's way out of a trap (Mailer, 1968, p. 86). It is not only the last resort in the bargaining spectrum but also a potentiality or a threat which does in fact change the bargaining equation itself. In a sense, it is the ultimate test of viability of values and customary behavior.

To sketch the complex systems of political change, it will be necessary to cut across many disciplines of the behavioral sciences. Our aim is an integrated and compelling model of a process of which violence is an integral part. Like heckling, harassing demonstrations, and strong-arm political goons, even assassination as a political tactic can become commonplace, as war is today in the relations between nation-states. We need to understand the grave danger that violence may replace orderly politics, and the process that permits it to, if we hope to do something about it, to reverse the present trend, and to avoid avoidable recurrences. The propositions, questions, and suggestions that follow in this book aim at conceptual clarity and interrelatedness and seek to provoke ideas and reflection; they are not final conclusions. In offering this theory of political behavior I have tried, following the guidance of Harold D. Lasswell, to elicit the broadest possible "patterns of variables whose inner actions constitute the relevant political institution" (Lasswell, 1963, p. 93).

Some Definitions

Definitions are the building blocks of reasoning and discourse. They always contain elements of arbitrariness and of tautology. In addition, by limitation and selection they frequently control the statement of the problem and therefore imply the whole argument and its conclusions. In the view of symbolic logicians, theory, like pure mathematics, is nothing but an extended tautology, a closed system bounded by its own categories and certain rules of language. The only escape from enclosure lies in operational usefulness. As the tautology wends its way back to its starting point, it must elaborate enough symbols and representations of real things and reationships to give it verisimilitude and correspondence to the indicators and points of intervention in the universe it describes. In short, it is a cultural artifact, a tool whose truth and power emanate from its success in mediating between man and the part of his social and physical environment that is under study.

Much of philosophy and the social sciences deals with "power," "violence," "force," and the nature and functions of the state and its police power.[1] *Power* is the most overworked and ill-defined word in political discourse. It can be defined most concretely in physical terms: Power is the application of energy to do work. It is the man or machine moving a mass from here to there. At a higher level of abstraction, power is the ability to direct energy to modify or control the environment, to express values (designs, goals, etc.) through intervention in the configuration of things. In terms of the social environment, power may be viewed as the ability to direct human energy (i.e., attitudes and behavior) to express or realize certain values by the organization and use, modification and control of both physical and human (i.e., behavior itself) materials (Mumford, 1966, pp. 234-62; Walter, 1964, p. 350).

The existence and use of social power and its organizational results (behavior norms, social institutions, public policies, attitudes, etc.) may be described as arising from biological necessity.

---

[1] See Walter, 1964, pp. 350–55; Oppenheim, 1961; Russell, 1962; Homans, 1961; Emmet, 54 (1954), 13; Ortega y Gasset, 1946, pp. 34–35; Tillich, 1961, esp. pp. 7–13; Weber, 1947; and Simmel, 1955.

Mumford and others suggest that the task of elaborating the social order is the primary task of human groups; the most elemental human drive toward creativity, ritual, and play gives rise to manners, ceremony, social systems, inventions, and technologies (Mumford, 1966, p. 3). In human terms, at the brute level of physical operations, power lies in one man's ability to restrain, transport, immobilize, injure, or destroy his fellow. Such a form of power cannot practically serve as a normal means of regulating intragroup relations; it conflicts with the very values which sustain life, those of mutual adaptation and collaboration against a hostile environment, physical or human. The functions of social forms and the political socialization of the individual aim to minimize and control such dysfunctional uses of power, replacing them with norms of behavior which foster the positive, ongoing values of group life.

Raw physical power becomes functional and *legitimate* in the hands of some kind of centralized authority as a means of providing internal and external security. Domestic, politically socialized power is transmuted into indirect forms manifested by prestige, influence, property-holding, skill, class or caste, physical beauty, and the like. The constituted authority structure holds a legitimate monopoly of the means of physical power in order to enforce the norms of social relationships, rights and responsibilities, procedures for political change, conduct and mediation of private and public bargaining, and exchange of values among individuals and groups by means of attenuated and socialized forms of indirect and decentralized power.

Force can be viewed as the reserve capability and means of exercising physical power. In a well-ordered, stable society, the possession and use of force by private individuals must be defensive only, and its possession and use by the state an explicit means of supporting the authority of the system to persuade, deter, or coerce. Force then amounts to a *threat* of violence or counterviolence. If violence is actually used, it may constitute merely a demonstration of force, a symbolic and limited act to give the capability and determination of further action enough credibility to induce deterrence or compliance at minimum cost and risk and with minimum provocation of ancillary fear and resistance (Blau, 1966, pp. 19-24).

Violence can be unambiguously defined as the most direct and severe form of physical power. It is force in action. Its use is a continuation of bargaining begun by other means, whether it is used by the state, by private groups, or by persons. All the attenuated politically socialized forms of indirect power are brushed aside. The threat of force becomes action, inching from forms of demonstration and continued bargaining into a direct test of relative power by actual mutual attack and defense. Bargaining, inducement, coercion, and possible accommodation now hang upon tactical and strategic weakness and advantage, the shifting conditions of maneuver and battle. Yet, short of the total collapse or destruction of the means of struggle on one side, the element of bargaining, the continuous assessment of capabilities, risks, and costs, is not suspended in the movement toward eventual accommodation. Power in the sense of raw violence, defense, and counterviolence is always in the process of measurement, which at some point of respite becomes the provisional basis for political settlement.

A situation reduced to this extreme may well preserve survival values and future bargaining power even for the weaker antagonists. As in all things, there is an economy of the use of force in terms of cost, risk, and benefits, whether for nation-states or for disaffected minorities. The capability and determination to exact unacceptable cost from the enemy, even at great cost to oneself, may be the only means by which a small nation or minority group can maintain respect for its independence, values, demands, and political bargaining power, while avoiding the escalation of violence to extreme limits. The weak may lose, but they may also win by testing the cost-risk-benefit constraints of the strong; in any case, they may have no choice. For both sides risk arises from the loss of ability to limit, control, or predict the dynamics of a confrontation crisis. This is especially true of a domestic confrontation in which groups have greater proximity, and thus more occasion for random actions, and less formal organization and discipline.

The common definitions of violence (uncontrolled and dysfunctional) and force (controlled and legitimate) we find inadequate (see Sorel, 1905, 1961). The distinctions among capability, threat, and demonstration are more widely applicable and therefore more useful. *Force* equals capability and threat of action; *violence* equals demonstration of force tending toward counterdemonstration and escalation, or toward containment and settlement. Thus, force and violence merge imperceptibly. The actual demonstration (force in action) must occur from time to time to give credibility to its threatened use or outbreak; in this way the threat gains efficacy as an instrument of social and political change or control.

Political motives may be seen in all kinds of behavior—including all acts of violence. What is needed is a broad definition which emphasizes the continuity of extreme behavior and normative behavior. I offer seven categories that are relevant to all forms of political behavior:

1. Object or victim (toward which or whom the behavior is directed)
2. Implementation (the way the act is carried out)
3. Motivation (deep or superficial, calculated or impulsive, etc.)
4. Association (lone act, small or large conspiratorial group, etc.)
5. Organization of the activity (professional assassin, leaders and underlings, hapless actor induced by threat or pressure of others, etc.)
6. Culture pattern (perception or assertion of normative pattern of political behavior)
7. Political impact and effects

Trying to cover all these aspects, one may state a definition of political violence: *acts of disruption, destruction, injury whose purpose, choice of targets or victims, surrounding circumstances, implementation, and/or effects have political significance, that is, tend to modify the behavior of others in a bargaining situation that has consequences for the social system.*

The categories of this definition will fit any kind of behavior, political or criminal, yet they force upon us distinctions which separate political behavior from all acts of violence which lack significant political dimensions. This definition makes it possible to differentiate among acts of violence and to relate them to "threats, capabilities, and attempts," all of which may have political significance. It also enables one to narrow every kind of special case and to require a clear description of key factors. It emphasizes the impact and consequences of acts, the exploitation of outcomes by actors and others which may endow the activity with its most important political character. By using general categories applicable to all political behavior, it opens the way to comparative analysis.

There is no reason, for example, for not dealing with political murder when it occurs within small political groups, formal or informal, having the same pattern and significance at that level of social organization as an assassination of national or international scope may have. Throughout the political and social structure, threats and acts of violence may be comparable in terms of intending or acquiring a purposive political effect. This includes retributive feuds and murder chains, riots, provocative demonstrations, counterdemonstrations, acts of deterrence, compellence, enforcement, and punishment; warfare among tribal elites, reprisals, and rudimentary systems of self-help justice; symbolic, ritual, or ceremonial acts aimed at diverting the real thing by means of a substitute that has similar effects; violence and threats of violence as a form of "propaganda of the act"; as a demonstration of group unity or individual commitment, or as a test of these qualities in rival groups; as a demand for attention from a larger audience; as a claim, assertion, and testing of legitimacy; as an act of enforcing and maintaining authority; as a provocation falsely blamed on innocent groups in order to justify actions against them; as retaliation or reprisal in a bargaining relationship that moves toward settlement; as a method of terror; as a way of forcing confrontation on other issues; or as a way of avoiding such confrontation by diverting attention; as an expression and measure of group or individual commitment; as a test of the manhood and loyalty of new recruits; as a method of precipitating revolutionary conditions; and so on.

This list suggests the functional continuities that exist in threats and acts of violence encompassed by our definition. Through its categories, one can deal with otherwise meaningless and isolated acts of desperate individuals. Marginal individuals inhabit a world in which fantasy endows them with the same legitimacy and purposefulness that give meaning to the policy uses of violence by organized groups; and it becomes more useful to understand how political groups use the psychotic individual or exploit his actions in their own interests than to dwell upon the etiology of individual illness.

Apparently meaningless acts of violence must be studied as part of the continuum of political behavior. It is always difficult to separate the assassin's individualized motives, intentions, and purposes from the social process of which his act is a part. Indeed, it is not necessary to do so; in fact it is more helpful and probably more realistic to admit a wide variety of motives, including those which may be contradictory: the individual's problems and values, his relationship, aspiration, or sense of identity with other groups and individuals, his structure of loyalties (including some that are divided), his post hoc rationalizations, and so on. There is a kind of arbitrariness about who commits a political act and for what reasons. Like the simultaneity of invention, when a need exists, many rise, from separate life situations, to fill it. The historical record shows many assassination plots smoldering at approximately the same time but in different places and frequently with different motives. In a sense, the actors of violent events are always instruments of larger dynamic relationships; this fact may suggest the path to a political analysis of extremism and political violence.

Some Central Themes

One may summarize the central themes of this book:

1. The political components of behavior are generically the same in all groups from the family to the world's society of nations, and the dynamics work in much the same way within each level of the organizational hierarchy.
2. In all political arenas, the causal processes and functions of violence are parallel.
3. Sheer unproductive power to inflict pain and grief is part of a bargaining process and, while ambiguous in its use, is often used.
4. The incidence of group violence increases as groups assume semi-sovereign functions as a challenge to or substitute for the weakened legitimacy of the state.

5. Beneath all the forms of polite society lies a stratum of potential violence which constitutes the ultimate test of the viability of social groups and institutions.

We begin with the premise that society is inherently composed of competitive individuals and groups, all struggling to maintain or advance their advantages by a wide variety of means. Change is endemic, and men must be seen as adopting peaceful or violent means to participate in and adjust to it; social action always moves along a continuum between violence and nonviolence simply because social life is dynamic. Under what we call "stable conditions," the general change-generating competition is carried on in a low key, through the nation's legal-political organs in a continuous and traditionally legitimized manner. Under what we call "unstable conditions," bargaining among interest groups is sometimes intensified to the point of violence (the militant challenge) and counterviolence (the governmental defense of a given interest coalition).

In the context of heightened instability; deviant or criminal groups (also pursuing their interests as they see them) and groups favoring violence tend to increase in number and to enlarge the quantity and range of their activity. Thus; "disorder," "deviance," and "breakdown" appear to accompany the rise of militant political challengers. However, these cannot be isolated from society's "normal" state; rather, they are an extension of it. Their appearance merely indicates that the bargaining and change process is being intensified and carried on by other means.

When groups favoring violent means of pressing interest claims on society gain informal legitimacy, they provide models of behavior for others. The assassin—one such type—shows himself when the social bargaining process is being carried on violently. Thus, political assassination is the outcome of social dynamics at a particular point when change cannot be structured by established legal-political organs; it is not a "unique," "abnormal," or "insane" event. "Stability" and "disorder" as inherently connected, not as discrete states of being but as routine social processes.

Conflict is an essential aspect of growth, one that we can neither fully control nor prevent, nor should we wish to do so. Social life exhibits a strong strain toward humanizing power and dampening extreme oscillations of change. History clearly demonstrates that societies can and do recover and even profit from seizures and disasters, that soldiers returning from brutal wars can be gentle, that extreme behavior is selective and politically limited under all but the most catastrophic conditions.

To unlearn is more difficult than to learn; and it seems that the task of breaking up rigid cognitive structures and reassembling them into a new synthesis cannot, as a rule, be performed in the full daylight of the conscious, rational mind. . . .

Koestler, 1967, p. 179

A CRITIQUE OF COMMON THEORIES

2

Dealing with a social problem requires having a theory about its causes. Such theories are provisional; their ultimate test lies in the success or failure of social policies formulated under their guidelines. Various theories have been adduced to explain the new politics of violence. Some of the least satisfactory are the most widely embraced; the fervor and frequency with which they are reiterated accent the fact that they are spurious and unconvincing.

Riffraff and Reds

Among the most loudly argued theories is the notion that Communists or "outside agitators" with links to Hanoi, Peking, Havana, if not Moscow, are behind every serious act of disruption and collision. Even if these conspirators do not incite and control events, they are always present to exploit, manipulate, and some-

19

how energize rioters and militant demonstrators, through some mysterious power which only Communists possess. The real Communists in America, aging, fuddy-duddy, and discredited, are delighted to accept the accolades thus freely given them by mayors and police chiefs.

This theory need not long detain us. But some of its variations have been seriously submitted by the McCone Commission (which studied the 1965 Watts riot) and by other responsible people: "senseless and meaningless outburst," treasonous acts of psychopaths bent on the destruction of the American system, revolt of the downtrodden of the urban ghetto who have little to lose by turning to violence. This collection of diagnoses is usually referred to as the *riffraff theory.* The public and its officials find it easy to label group violence as criminal—that is, fundamentally and unconditionally illegitimate—or meaningless. "Such an interpretation makes it easier for them to deal with the dark, to rationalize the otherwise inexplicable, and to obviate the necessity to feel guilty about the society's failure to deal with the underlying causes of the violence in the ghetto" (Masotti, 1967, p. 1).

The riffraff theory maintains that a kind of spontaneous contagion enables incorrigible mischief-makers and no-gooders to unleash uncontrolled escalations, sweeping responsible and law-abiding bystanders into a vortex of violence. It does not adequately account for the process by which the riffraff, if indeed that is what they are, achieve legitimacy and leadership roles. Social contagion cannot be viewed as automatic and independent of other variables. Nor can it be persuasively argued that acts of extremism are idiosyncratic, that is, accountable solely in terms of highly personalized individual impulses and personalities, with little significance in terms of group conflict and political bargaining. Such a view evades the question of why some individual emotional seizures are amplified to social scale, while others are not.

At the core of the riffraff theory are three themes that are widely taken for granted by American public opinion. First is the notion that only an infinitesimal fraction of the black population (only two percent according to some, including several prominent Negro moderates, and one percent according to others) actively participated in the riots of the 1960s. Second is the idea that the rioters, far from being representative of the Negro community, were principally the unattached, the juvenile, the unskilled, the unemployed, the uprooted, the criminal—and outside agitators. And third, the overwhelming majority of the Negro population, it is held, unequivocally opposed and deplored the riots (Fogelson and Hill, 1968, p. 222).

All studies of American ghetto riots in the sixties dispute these three assumptions. They indicate that very substantial numbers of people participated actively in the riots in some capacity, in most cases well over 15 percent. Surveys of the Negro community in Watts showed well over half of those interviewed expressing support and understanding for the actions of the rioters. The actual proportion of sympathizers is assumed to be higher, since many respondents might well have been unwilling to admit their positions to an interviewer. Finally, virtually all the studies indicate that the leaders and the participants were largely indigenous to the riot communities and saw their actions as a justifiable form of protest. They and most blacks interviewed thought that the violent outbursts would work favorably to modify the relation of the ghetto to the white majority power structure (Tomlinson, 1968, p. 2). A recent study by the Institute for Communication Research, Stanford University, found that 72 percent of "high-income" Negroes thought the urban riots were positive factors of social protest and effective in changing slum conditions (Funkhouser and Maccoby, *New York Times*, December 16, 1968, p. 41).

". . . American as Cherry Pie!"

The uniqueness of the American experience is often used to explain or justify a high incidence of political and personal violence. It is held that the nation's history is saturated with blood and violence, in the conquest first of the Indians and then of the frontier.

In an idealized version the frontiersman is seen as a law unto himself. The frontier created the myths of unlimited and equal opportunity, of self-reliance and self-help, and the tradition of keeping and bearing arms. As the frontier closed, people rushed to the cities, bringing with them the culture of Dodge City shoot-outs, gun-slinging, gangsterism, and vigilantism (see Elliott, 1952, p. 273). Slavery, too, was a system based on violence, just as was colonial subjugation of the emancipated slaves, in both North and South, down to the present. The whole history of property rights, labor-management relations, interstate disputes, and nationality, religious, and racial relations has been steeped in violence. Politics has never been free from gangland wars, assassinations, riots of every variety. In short, according to the *frontier theory*, America presents a unique cultural setting which, despite lip service to peaceable democratic institutions, legitimizes and induces violent behavior.

Closely related to this hypothesis is the *gun theory*, which argues that the prevalence of privately owned weapons in itself increases the use of guns for political purposes, for assassination, sniping, and shoot-outs with the police, that it leads to private paramilitary groups like the white Minute Men or the black Deacons of Justice.

Both theories contain elements of truth. Their differences are most evident in the remedies they suggest and the political tactics they are used to justify. Admirers of the gun theory advocate strong federal gun control and regulation of gun traffic. The American frontier school generally argues for more radical protest tactics or excuses the use of such tactics.

Certainly the tradition of possessing and bearing arms is wide-spread, and a large number of deaths can be laid to guns. In 1968, twenty thousand people died from the use of firearms in homicides, suicides, and accidents, an average of fifty people each day, or one every thirty minutes. Proper gun control, it is said, might have prevented the assassination chain that took the lives of the Kennedy brothers, Martin Luther King, Viola Liuzzo, and others. The new phase of Mau Mau terrorism against policemen would not exist if sniper rifles were not so readily available.

There is considerable justice in this position. The statistics of killings both by and of policemen tend to confirm it. In England, the absence of guns in the hands of police has discouraged professional thieves and burglars from bearing arms. Woundings and killings attendant upon arrest have been drastically fewer than in America, where any thief or purse-snatcher may try to anticipate the police by shooting first, and vice versa. However, the British have recently found it necessary to arm London police because of the Americanization of professional crime.

The gun theory is attractive. If true, it seems to provide an area in which simple legislation can drastically diminish the level of deadly violence. But there are difficulties in this approach. How could we control arms traffic without imposing repressive and repugnant measures of police surveillance upon the whole society? How could we deal with the high incidence of violence perpetrated with such weapons as ice picks, bricks, and kitchen knives? The evidence is not fully convincing that the ubiquity of guns in itself encourages their use in crime, personal attacks, and political action. The gun theory echoes a now discredited view of the role of armaments in international conflict. The view that an armaments race inevitably leads to war, which enjoyed great currency during the isolationist period between the world wars, has been generally discarded in the face of the necessity for maintaining permanent diplomacy that has been the fate of the United States since World War II. Students of military strategy generally agree that a balance of arms induces not adventurism but restraint, that nuclear parity brings about a kind of de facto mutual deterrence both in the use of these weapons and in diplomatic threats of their use. The kind of diplomacy which may lead to war is not generated by arms and arms races, but rather the other way around: weapons are a symptom and an instrument of diplomatic conflict, not the cause. The same may be applied to the prevalence of guns and arms races within American society.

The very fact that ghettos and suburbs are arming themselves is creating a higher level of risk and danger; however, rather than leading to open warfare, it may just as well lead to mutual deter-

more fighting occurs between people who make love than between
those who do not, and a great deal more love is made in the course
of the social excitement of wartime. On the basis of the evidence,
one may well argue that sexual indifference, impassivity in human
relations, would do more to reduce the statistics of murderous
assault than the opposite. Moreover, people tend to kill each other
less frequently when they are engaged in killing foreigners, and vice
versa.

The McLuhan Thesis

Sociologists have long given great weight to cultural diffusion,
imitation, mimicry, and contagion as mechanisms by which behavior change is transmitted through social groups and societies. Almost every theory of contemporary political violence subsumes
such a transmittal mechanism at work, regardless of the specific
causes and motivations which bring about the innovative norm and
reinforce its spread to other groups.

At this point, we are concerned with Marshall McLuhan's thesis
that electronic communications are transforming and retribalizing
society, inducing a new immediacy of human contact and a violent
revolution of individual consciousness.

In McLuhan's words, "Today electronics and automation make
mandatory that everybody adjust to the vast global environment as
if it were his little home town" (McLuhan, 1968, p. 11). The instan-
taneous electronic global village ties all its members into a single
web of interacting, vibrating hearts and souls. The poor, the young,
and the black are no longer invisible to the great middle majority,
and the closed lines of communication of the old printed media
(which tended to follow and maintain caste and class structures) no
longer exclude anyone. "You are there, and they are here!" The
most scabrous cold-water tenement, lacking books, newspapers, or
print of any kind, has television sets going day and night in every
flat. Ghetto teen-agers have transistor radios glued to their ears.
The black child wonders why his skin is not "flesh-colored," to
match the Bandaids—or why Bandaids are not made in his flesh

color. The census bureau reported that 87 percent of nonwhite households have television sets; 94 percent of white households have them. A *Washington Post* survey indicated that Negro readership of newspapers is only half that of whites.

It is argued that the media, particularly television, create a stage upon which demonstrators and rioters carry out a new art form which might be called "street theater." The protesters play to the cameras, quickly learning how to do this with great effect, provoking and entrapping city authorities, university administrators, and police into playing exactly the roles and speaking the lines called for by the dissidents' script.

Abbie Hoffman, the Yippie leader of the 1968 Chicago riots, was explicit in his strategy of image-making, applying all the lessons of Madison Avenue as methods of packaging and selling confrontation: ". . . I fight through the jungle of TV, you see. . . . It's all in terms of disrupting the image, the image of a democratic society being run very peacefully and orderly and everything according to business" (*Milwaukee Sentinel*, December 2, 1968, p. 3). The elaborate array of grandiose threats (to dump LSD in the city's water supply, for example) was part of the script, designed to condition authorities and demonstrators for the parts the leaders hoped they would play. Chicago's Mayor Richard Daley, in the city's television special designed to defend police actions ("How Many Trees Do They Plant?"), argued that the police were not to blame if the demonstrators sought to incite certain reactions and were accommodated.

In its vulgar form, this theory has been offered in connection with almost every major violent event in the last decade. The mayors of Birmingham and Selma both blame the unblinking eye of the television camera for massive and provocative demonstrations against prevailing authorities. In Chicago, a number of newsmen observed how quickly a throng of demonstrators gathered when a television camera came into sight. One cameraman exclaimed, "Give me enough cameras, and I'll take over the world!" The violence of the police is often directed not only at peaceful or violent demonstrators but also at reporters and cameramen and their equipment.

Violence is held to be a kind of energizing human electricity, the link to electrical signals and current.[2] The television screen, McLuhan says, has changed the balance of our senses. Unlike the theater, the printed word, or the movie screen (the latter being merely a variety of theater), the television tube minimizes the communicator's programming and predigestion of experiences. In all the older media, the editor, writer, actor, director can structure the communication of experience to make it conform to images reflecting his own ways of reacting and absorbing, ways that usually are consensualist and tend to reinforce the status quo. Consequently, the older media tended by and large to maintain social distance and insularity in the vision of reality transmitted differentially to social groups.

"The medium is the message" expresses the fact that the *forms* of communication themselves have a central and primary effect on the kinds of things that are communicated. The intrusion of television, especially documentaries, news, and live coverage, makes us suddenly and distressingly aware of realities for which we lack insulation and prescribed social images. There is no literacy gap to reinforce existing institutions; every watcher sees all kinds of things not intended or prepared for him. The commentator, the film and videotape editor, the cameraman who points the electronic eye, the director who selects the product of many cameras—all strive to do the traditional filtering of the older media. But they fail because their efforts to program and structure the experience in accord with yesterday's clichés and norms is imperfect.

Television, with its immediacy of news coverage, transmits a vast amount of raw, undigested experience to which people react, not according to safe and recognizable categories, but in direct and wholly unpredictable ways. The world becomes a tribal village. The picture is not on the screen; rather, the beam of light goes to the very brain of the viewer as a kind of first-hand experience, identical in effect to his face-to-face experiences. Tribal immediacy, spon-

---

[2] As this huge new arm—electronic communications and computers—reaches out into the community, "it is inevitable that it will proliferate spastic behavior for some time to come. The attempt to adapt the new computer to the diversity of older technologies creates a great deficiency of feedback" (McLuhan, 1968, p. 95).

taneity, and highly personal reaction to everything that is happening throughout the world extends the group and the self in unprecedented ways. The entire locked-in audience reacts to far-flung events, including wars, riots, and assassinations, with untutored nakedness. Geographical distance and perspective, the buffers of human relations in complex societies, disappear, and all things everywhere reach, involve, and threaten the entire audience.

Government policy, McLuhan suggests, can no longer separate killing for policy reasons abroad from killing at home. Vietnams become impossible because the whole nation experiences them simultaneously and completely. The viewer looks into the face of a wounded Viet Cong and sees a man. He looks into the face of a president and reads a message entirely different from the man's words. Whatever official policy does in faraway places threatens and justifies similar behavior at home in every context of personal relations and domestic politics. Television, McLuhan proclaims, has eliminated the possibility of making careful separations and distinctions, as previous ages did, in order to specialize behavior norms to serve differentiated social functions. Now everyone is in on everything; all respond to all kinds of events in clusters of meaning that have nothing to do with official purposes and often conflict with them. A riot, demonstration, or act of police terrorism in Chicago has the same effect in Birmingham as if it had occurred there. Any provocative event creates a simultaneous and epidemic reaction throughout the country.

Social excitement and panic in the New York subway becomes social excitement in subways in Chicago, energizing and precipitating not only home-town muggers but also overreactive prevention and retaliation. The very simultaneity and sensitivity of the extended tribal village generates every variety of extremism, and predisposes extremists to seek exposure and an audience through the media in order to generalize and propagate their own acts.

In its hyperbolic form, the McLuhan thesis holds that electronic media are directly responsible for the incidence of personal and political violence, quite apart from all other kinds of factors that may predispose individuals toward tactics of confrontation. The dynamics of the electronic media compels individuals and groups to seek exposure and attention by doing something different or new. They are forced to dramatize themselves by escalating sensation and inventing new tactics to maximize shock values. Four-letter words, nudism, public fornication, and the like are justified as forms of political protest in the competition for the attention, not of persons in the immediate vicinity, but of the media. Ersatz and pseudo events and manipulated happenings assume political significance and power that they never had in the rationalistic, linear clichés of pre-video media. Even the advertising men look to the inventors of simultaneity in seeking to market goods and ideas.

The least inhibited youths become the dominant innovators because they are the freshest and most spontaneous product of the video age. Everything becomes possible and "anything goes" as those who are least programmed by the clichés and inhibitions of the past respond to and exploit a new possibility of instant revolution in every area of life and in all institutions.

This doctrine attracts not only beseiged public officials who require a scapegoat but also the media men themselves, for whom it tends to confirm and inflate their claims of importance—and their revenues. If the thesis were valid, the solution to confrontation politics, extremism, and violence would lie in more perfect control of the media in the interests of public policy and, conversely, more attention to the example set by public policy. Interview shows, documentaries, and news would have to be more competently tailored to avoid unintended communications which arise from the simultaneity, rawness, and immediacy of the tube. Situation comedies, old movies, and straight news broadcasting might deprive us of what little breath of reality now comes across the airwaves.

Fortunately, the problem is not that simple, and the power structure would have nothing to gain by trying to suppress the pluralistic nature of present media coverage. First of all, the contagion phenomenon is real. Imitation, fadism, mimicry are fundamental to the process of socialization. They are how we learn from each others' experience, how we test and prove new values and new behavior. A violent march anywhere tends to generate violent marches elsewhere. This was true not only before television but also before radio and even before newspapers. Channels of communication gain their credibility not by their mere existence or ubiquity but by the immemorial individual test of confidence and trust that arises out of need-satisfaction and meaningfulness. The real coin of communication is validated by the old fundamental usages.

Word of mouth between people who serve each other's needs remains the most powerful and sometimes the most rapid form of communication (in terms of response). Under McLuhan's hypothesis, it is incredible that Christianity could revolutionize the Roman Empire; or that the American, French, and Russian revolutions, with their awkward handbills and posters, could have occurred at all. The receiver of electronic communications edits the content of the message in accordance with his own structures, images, predispositions, and needs, just as he always has edited the editors, the commentators, and the Madison Avenue boys. Even the best-conceived propaganda and the most delicate soft sell can be edited out by the viewer as the electronic beam scans his retinas. What is transmitted to the mind is meaningful in terms of what is already there. Interest, attention, and the predisposition to react in certain ways are not spontaneously effected or locked in equally to every communication.

The immemorial human relations of individual and group experience, affiliation and loyalty, identification with social values and perceptions of self-interest are commingled in that vast complexity that underlies all political reality, the modern as well as the ancient. People have always reacted to events in terms of their own needs and problems and their social identities, not in terms of the self-serving construction placed upon events by those who may communicate them. Receptivity to certain kinds of experience and a predisposition to interpret and react in certain ways are much more basic than the precise form or vehicle of communication. When violent demonstrations proliferated in response to the assassination of Martin Luther King, it was not because of the televised funeral; it was because of what Martin Luther King's life and actions meant to the lives and actions of those who loved and hated him. Events that reflect conflict tend to be generalized when others identify with the conflict. When this condition does not exist, there is no automatic generation of imitative behavior.

The media managers have an uncanny feeling for the kinds of experience that will arrest the attention of large groups of people. While educators and churchmen may disapprove of the disproportionate attention given to sensational, violent acts, while mayors and police chiefs may not be pleased by scrutiny of their treatment of minorities, the news media are attracted to these frontiers of social change for the same reasons that the general audience is interested in them. All people select and abstract from the noisy buzz of communications (indeed, from all sense data) the categories and content that serve their individual purposes. Society has a more urgent need to know about one person killed crossing a street than about thousands who crossed safely. News men and editors are as much a part of conflict groups and have as much stake in the changing institutions as anyone. Where people are willing to take grave risks, where social institutions are threatened, where disruptive or self-destructive behavior proliferates—these are the real frontiers of social change where values are struggling to be born or to die. Human relations, conflict, situations that embarrass or compromise the powerful, the character of men, and the universal comedy and tragedy of real lives—these are the things closest to all people. These are not abstractions of public policy, but rather "what's happening" and "where it's at." Reports of crime and criminality, suicide and murder, strikes and divorces—these are real. All the rest are self-serving abstractions and ideologies which buffer and conceal the dimensions of trauma in society.

News of the Columbia University revolt in the spring of 1968 was transmitted to other campuses throughout the country not only by Huntley and Brinkley. Personal couriers working through student and church groups, in letters and newspapers, communicated rumors, lies, and imaginative constructions by all sorts of individuals to many kinds of audiences. Imitative outbreaks proliferated because many people living with related problems could use the information in some way. The outcome of any high-risk bargaining engagement is significantly interesting to all engaged in similar situations, since the engagement may provide a model for both tactics and outcomes. A powerful model in fact tends to influence behavior and outcomes symbolically, making unnecessary the repetition of escalated risk-taking. Thus, S.I. Hayakawa and Governor Reagan sought a showdown at San Francisco State College in order to create a new model which could refute the symbolic efficacy of the Columbia and Berkeley models—thereby discouraging future tactics of disruption.

When someone goes over the edge at one place, his act tends to excite conflict elsewhere and to force others over the edge. Fads of suicide, of lynching, of demonstrations, sit-ins, and so on reflect adaptive reinforcement of behavior. Communication is the link; but the content of the event and its adaptability to other situations are what bring some kinds of faddist behavior, but not others, to epidemic proportions. In addition, the same process encompasses built-in correctives and counterforces by those who are threatened by a specific wave of mimicry. Not the media but the substratum of bargaining among individuals and social groups has always been the chief factor in shaping and changing human societies. One fad peters out in a few weeks and another becomes a permanent way of life, while the media sometimes help, sometimes resist, sometimes tag along for their own purposes.

Violence may under certain circumstances prove an adaptive method of inducing political action. Television coverage may not only encourage extremism; it may, on the contrary, discourage it by providing a forum at less risk. Were the common forum of the nation's psychic life to exclude certain social groups or values, it would force political change into even more extreme tactics in the search for attention and audiences. (Here we see the wisdom of the Bill of Rights which guarantees the right to petition, hire a hall for a meeting, demonstrate peacefully in the public streets, however unpopular the occasion may be.) The media may facilitate communications; they may also have just the opposite effect. When they are misused, they sacrifice their credibility in the interests of the advertising dollar, entertainment, or the propaganda interests of government or powerful economic groups. People then may not believe even what is communicated honestly and not respond to it. The debasement of the coin of public communication is a much more dangerous and subversive tendency than is exuberant confrontation politics.

Censorship or voluntary agreements to suppress the news serve only to discredit the media and to drive communications underground. They simply do not work. People have never been fully dependent on any single medium of information. The raising of artificial barriers to information forces greater risk-taking as a means of obtaining public attention, entrains a vast proliferation of all the informal means by which people and groups customarily communicate and concert their reactions to events, and prompts futile self-defeating attempts by the powerful to impose the same control on informal media. As a link between social groups, television is much preferable to the trappings of underground committees of correspondence and courier networks and their deepening alienation. The truth is that insurgents willing to take risks have considerable freedom of action in defining the issues at stake and in projecting their own self-serving rationales of conflict to the public. This advantage is the very nature of direct action techniques; it gives them whatever efficacy they have. Efforts to deny this advantage by controlling information can serve only to undermine the legitimacy of formal authority and thereby to enhance the advantages of the dissidents.

Since informal communication networks cannot be eliminated, formal authority has more to gain by accepting media coverage as an opportunity to demonstrate its own viability, countering the insurgents with their own weapons, setting an example by not playing the demonstrators' game. In a study of insurrections in underdeveloped countries, Lucian W. Pye writes, "Government's behavior is usually the test people employ to judge the credibility of insurgent's claims. A government can expect to be judged according to its grasp of reality, its capability of coping with the threat, its chances of controlling the future—in sum, its ability to act as a sovereign authority should in preserving its authority" (Pye, 1968, p. 168). Because the dissidents hold the initiative, to act as they should is an exceedingly difficult task for public authorities and for the police. But it is not impossible. Adequate force can remain passive, meeting force with force in kind and degree, and never escalating the conflict above the degree of cost-risk imposed by the demonstrators.

Beyond the confrontation itself, credibility and legitimacy must be sought by all the forces of the community through constructive political leadership. All the routes of democratic access should be widened to ensure the transmutation of conflict from "street theater" to every kind of social and political forum that can be made available for the conduct and management of social bargaining. If television and radio are indeed the significant forums of our times, more coverage, not less, is required to contain destructive violence. Public attention, which has a gift for knowing "where it's at" in the informal polity, will be served by more coverage. Indeed, it should be served in the multitude of ways available to many competing centers of media control; such competition prevents the much greater danger involved in blanketing the information channels with the wishful thinking of beseiged and anxious men in television studios, city hall, or the White House.

Critics who would make a scapegoat of the media are grasping at a partial truth. New technology does modify the functional significance of certain kinds of behavior by providing new routes and means of expression. Street theater may become an institutionalized ritual of social conflict, which much evidence suggests is happening. Like the ritualization of conflict in the forms of panty raids, stadium brawls climaxing football games, gang fights at the neighborhood dance, New Year's Eve mischief, and the like, such an institution may contain wholly constructive elements. Stylized violence in front of a television camera may have an augmented and amplified effect in changing attitudes and bargaining relationships throughout the country. It may even be that cultivation of street theater is a good and readily available means of limiting and controlling dangerous escalations, providing the formal authorities have their own script for such happenings and have trained the police to countertactics designed to limit violence.

Ritual violence is a safety valve and a catharsis. If it is too much feared, it is because the legitimacy of formal institutions is already insecure. Public authority must accept the inevitability of the challenge; it must seek to dramatize its legitimacy by using the media as effectively as do those who demonstrate or riot.

Return of the Killer Instinct

A current vogue posits a killer instinct which man inherits from subhuman ancestors. Tangled in his genes is a program for the fang and claw. Social institutions must vent, repress, and contain his fixed dosage of murderous potential. When institutions fail, whatever the cause, the gleeful, blood-thirsty caveman in each of us breaks out in search of a target and a victim.

This new version of Social Darwinism has re-emerged during the last few years, being represented by the writings of Konrad Lorenz (*On Aggression*), Robert Ardrey (*The Territorial Imperative*), and others. This view discovers that men are violently aggressive through genetic instinct. Evidence drawn from animal behavior studies is used to suggest that men will kill and maim at every opportunity and can be socialized only by coercion and state power. The confrontation politics of our time makes this theory immensely popular.[3] It is embraced by those who offer police power and larger jails as the solution to all disruptive behavior, and by those for whom it justifies a sense of inevitability and helplessness. Ardrey writes:

We are Cain's children. The union of the enlarging brain and the carnivorous way produced man as a genetic possibility. The tightly packed weapons of the predator form the highest, final, and most immediate foundation on which we stand. . . .

---

[3] It achieves an appearance of plausibility because, in the words of Ashley Montagu, it appears to have the support of "scientific learning, observation, discoveries, experiments, facts, and authorities." In addition, the proponents "are able and eloquent writers" whose "error, tendentiousness, and prejudice" has so far escaped check and control by other scientists from the relevant fields (Montagu, 1968, p. viii).

Man is a predator whose natural instinct is to kill with a weapon. The sudden addition of the enlarged brain to the equipment of an armed, already successful, predatory animal created not only the human being but also the human predicament . . . (Ardrey, 1967, p. 322).

The collectivist drive is derivative, he holds, and based on territoriality and defense. The primate has instincts that demand the maintenance and defense of territories, imposing an attitude of perpetual hostility toward the territorial neighbor, the formation of social bands as the principal means of survival, an attitude of amity and loyalty for the social partner, and varying but universal systems of dominance to ensure the efficiency of his social instrument and to promote the natural selection of the more fit from the less.

The *biological theory* of aggressiveness is similar in important respects to other theories that require an assertion that some or all men are inherently evil, violent, depraved, or monstrous in some respect. Each of these theories (riffraff or outside agitator, for example) has its own particular devil. A ready-made theoretical matrix, simple and dramatic, is available. Each group identifies the devils in question as "the cause of all our troubles," personified by whomever they are against. The formless specter in the corner, the bump in the night, news dealers, college professors, atheists, what you will—the pattern is the timeless one of black and white, good and evil, shifting blame from oneself to one's enemies, to one's genes, to one's stars. These are not theories at all, but rather ideologies of antagonism and fear.

The Ardrey-Lorenz view considers all men and human nature itself the enemy and the source of evil. It is an ideology of complacency, inaction, and defeatism because it justifies the inevitability of violence and the hopelessness of provisional remedies. Its promulgators do not really accept their own logic; they are forced to qualify and to improvise counterinstincts and contingent assumptions which tend to humanize and preserve human societies. The trap of their basic assumption, however, forces them to view the positive dimension as frail and undependable, subject to recurring ruptures through which predatory men will inevitably enter to maraud. Ardrey's case for the territorial imperative as a fundamental, genetically programmed drive of all species is full of unanswered questions. Assuming that every creature carries with him a bubble of ecological space essential to his existence and impenetrable as his flesh, one must nevertheless explain selective penetrations (love) and cohabitation (group life) which occur within hierarchical collective groups.

One of the founders of ethology, the study of animal behavior, is Dr. Nikolaas Tinbergen, Professor of Animal Behavior at Oxford University. With many other ethologists, he raises the issue that human aggressiveness has a fundamentally ambiguous character, that men tend to cohere in groups for which they develop intense loyalty. The ecological space of the individual tends to be violated selectively in all kinds of personal relationships, and to be submerged in the life of groups. Further, the degree of penetration among group members is structured; some claim and occupy more ecological space than others and possess differential rights of access to the common territory (*Tinbergen*, interview in *New York Times*, October 28, 1968, p. 6). Territoriality can be viewed as *learned* behavior, established through the successful aggressive display of groups occupying adjacent territory and bent on preventing loss of territory. In the same way, the extent of ecological space for the individual responds to his social bargaining role; it is defined through a learning process.

In his study of gorilla behavior in the wild, Schaller notes how functional and task-related is the social dominance hierarchy; it "does not cause strife and dissension, but promotes peace." Each member learns his place and role, enabling the nomadic food-gathering group to concert its actions (Schaller, 1964, pp. 131–32). Imitation, he found, was an important part of the process of socialization. He found insuperable difficulties in adopting a glib assumption of genetic instinct to account for most gorilla behavior:

. . . the apes—and this is true of other animals—are not under the total grip of their instincts. Learning and tradition play an important role in their lives, a role which is difficult to assess with precision in the wild, because each youngster gradually and unobtrusively learns the things that help it to fit into its group and its environment. Knowledge of food plants, route of travel, the proper way to respond to vocalizations and gestures—these and many other aspects are undoubtedly part of the gorilla's tradition, handed down as a result of individual experience from generation to generation and constituting a rudimentary form of culture (Schaller, 1964, p. 231).

The importance of tradition in animal society often becomes apparent only when a new trait appears. In recent years, for example, the blue tit, a European bird related to the American chickadee, acquired the remarkable habit of opening milk bottles on doorstops and taking the cream. This useful trait was apparently invented by a few tits in several localities, and it soon spread widely over western Europe. In the words of Ashley Montagu, the thesis of "innate depravity" is "unsound" and "dangerous" because "it perpetuates unsound views which justify, and even tend to sanction, violence which man is capable of learning, but which Mr. Ardrey erroneously believes to be inherited from man's Australopithecine ancestors" (Montagu, 1968, p. 6). Desmond Morris asserts that the ethological evidence is against the uncritical Ardrey-Lorenz view: "domination is the goal of aggression, not destruction, and basically we do not seem to differ from other species in this respect" (Morris, 1968, p. 175).

Deprivation, Access, Frustration

These three theories are closely related and similar in substance. The *deprivation theory* begins with a discussion of relative inequity, injustice, and inequality among social groups, postulating that the sharper the perception of inequity, the more intense the tactics of protest. The have-nots will look for occasions to attack the haves, and the greater the disparity between them, the larger will be the incentive for high-risk provocation. The deprivation theory is an ideology of social change on behalf of the underprivileged, but it does not contribute to our understanding of the dynamics of political behavior.

Studies of recent rioting indicate that disorientation, deprivation, and the problems of modern life, while important, are not sufficient explanation. Deprivation may provide drive and momentum, energizing and intensifying political behavior, but it does not determine which behavior norms will prove adaptive and reinforceable for some groups of the body politic. The view that violent outbreaks spring from deprivation neglects the obvious fact that such outbreaks occur selectively. Great deprivation may exist without such outbreaks, and outbreaks may occur without significant deprivation.

Differential access focuses upon the disparities in political influence and power as the most salient and influential factors. The less access to a remedy for its grievances a group has, the more violent it tends to become in demanding such access. By emphasizing structural inequalities as an independent variable, this view tends to place less weight upon the degree or intensity of particular political issues, dwelling instead upon relative social bargaining power as the key. The access theory admits a general congruence between power and deprivation, but dwells upon factors of social organization as more significant in stabilizing or upsetting public peace and tranquillity. Social disorganization and the rise of subcultures of violence are viewed more as results of differential access and unequal social power than as inevitable results of relative deprivation.[4]

Closely related to these theses is the psychological *theory of frustration-aggression*, which is frequently used to explain violent behavior. Frustration imposed by external sanctions or the physical world generates a cumulative rage that, at some point, breaks through in violent behavior. This theory is similar to the doctrine of repressed sexuality, but it broadens the range of drives that may be frustrated. One must be a very naive psychologist indeed to be satisfied with such a mechanistic explanation. Words begin to lose their meaning when they are constantly qualified by new variables or reinterpreted to mean something else.

---

[4] Cloward and Ohlin note that social norms, by defining legitimate practices, also implicitly define illegitimate practices. By calling attention to differential opportunity to become a criminal, they correct Merton's assumption that access to deviant behavior is uniformly available, regardless of position in the social structure. See Merton, 1957, chaps. 4 and 5; and Cloward and Ohlin, 1960.

Frustration can lead to breaking out in a rash, artistic sublimation and daydreaming, intense and vacuous masturbation, or other substitute outlets for energy. The social and psychological variables that constitute an external or internal block and intervene between frustration and aggression are too complex and diverse to be reduced to a simple reflex. Aggression is not necessarily adaptive; that is axiomatic in Skinnerian psychology. Frustrations that tend to reinforce a violent pattern of behavior must be understood as an adaptive, learned pattern for achieving values, even if the primary one becomes self-punishment. The simple frustration-aggression syndrome represents a very primitive state of the psychological art.

Coser points out that frustration does not of itself lead to questioning the legitimacy of vested interest (Coser, 1967, p. 31). Even a sharp conflict over institutionalized values that are denied to certain minorities can be stable when the elements of bargaining tend to reinforce differential frustration. American blacks lived a long time under a Constitution full of promise, yet they were relatively inured to frustration, deprivation, and lack of access. They did not achieve group consciousness, organization, and militancy until dominant power groups needed their labor—and national unity—to meet the requirements of war and diplomacy. Only then did these dominant groups show a readiness to yield to pressure for change, thus promising efficacy for attempts to bargain through organized institutions for a greater share of the values guaranteed by the Constitution. So long as the act of refusing to adjust to deprivation did not hold out any promise of having a good effect, it was possible for American blacks to adjust to disappointment, frustration, and lack of access to traditional bargaining.[5]

[5] "Physical force may be an important instrument in the enforcement of any deprivation. It is, however, intrinsic in the deprivation itself, particularly in deprivations of liberty. Although fines and taxation are backed by force, for example, the process of implementing such sanctions by taking over financial assets is ordinarily not a forcible one. If, however, an act of enforcement is challenged, the question of what to do in case of refusal to comply arises. This question can always lead to the problem of force, for resistance can be made effective . . . through such physical means as leaving the field commanded by ego or removing assets from it.The ultimate preventive of such evasion is force. Hence in a very broad sense we conclude that force is an "end-of-the-line" conception of a type of negative sanction that can be effective—in the context of deterrence, please note—when milder measures fail" (Parsons, 1964, p. 42).

Nevertheless the deprivation and access theories need to be taken seriously. While neither is fully adequate, both are relevant. Inequities, social disorganization, high-stress social conditions, high levels of excitement, and extreme situations for individuals and groups are elements in the bargaining process; hierarchical access to influence and affluence are universal features of organized societies. Even the most liberal and bountiful society disadvantages some persons and advantages others. Yet many societies have not been continuously torn apart by political extremism, revolution, and violence. Group deprivation and vast disparities of access have existed in relatively stable societies. A high degree of stress or repressive violence by the power elite may at some times enhance stability and at other times provoke counterviolence and collapse. A much better case can be made for the view that release from external stress or repression has frequently presaged the development of volatile political situations and the emergence of new demands and new constituencies in the political process. One cannot however, generalize this into a compelling doctrine of political violence, because it too is ambivalent. Political liberalization and economic progress may enhance stability and the development of peaceable political processes.

The main difficulty with all such theories arises from their ideological use. They are essentially doctrines of social reform which seek to exploit turbulence as a means for changing the norms of social systems and the power relationships between claimant groups. This is natural and inevitable, and the theories do indeed appear to be useful to large numbers of scholars, publicists, and politicians. This use of the theories is also controversial exactly because it distorts them tendentiously. However, one may share their value-base while still seeking a more objective analytic model. A student of political violence should not be forced to embrace frontlash as preferable to backlash; rather, he should see them as intrinsically related in a contest which, one hopes, can be moderated, at a lower level of cost-risk, with symbolic confrontation and tactics of display rather than tactics of destruction. At the same time, one can recognize that only the real potential of sudden escalation imposes restraints and limits demands. Such a potential may be the only means of enforcing mutual constraints, which in turn enable peaceable conciliation and adjustment to operate through political institutions like parties, legislatures, courts, and executive bureaucracies.

The crucial element that maintains ongoing human relations is the viability of all the parties to a bargaining engagement, their ability to pay each other off in kind, negatively if necessary, and positively so as to maximize values and the sweetness of group life. The negative formal and informal sanctions, up to and including violence, are therefore of the highest relevance to the quest for social order, stable, responsive and responsible government, and fruitful individual citizenship.

The popularity of reformist liberalism in the academic community gives the deprivation and access doctrines appeal and persuasiveness. But it also leads those threatened by social change to reject the social sciences, the professors, and the bureaucrats, undermining their effectiveness as objective brokers of social change. Many academics cannot understand why steps taken in accord with such theories frequently intensify the demands of the insurgents and escalate both frontlash and backlash; they cannot understand their being rejected by the new militant leaders, who consider reformist ideologies a variety of tokenism. They fail to grasp the dimensions of political bargaining reflected by cries of revolution and black power, which can be understood only in terms of bargaining equations underlying legalistic abstractions and economic improvements. It is the bargaining equations that determine whether progress toward reform will dampen extremism or encourage it.

Real bargaining does not limit itself to formal political institutions and legalistic formulas but flows under, over, and around these in actions and reactions among organized groups. The values and programs of groups are interdependent and reciprocal. Any group that has the power to work its will with impunity will escalate its impatience and its demands for institutionalized access and relative well-being. Similarly, the cost-risk conditions imposed by the responses and capabilities of other groups tend to limit demands as well as tactics. Revolutionary conditions characterize a state of uncertain bargaining relationships where the cost-risk equations have not been tested through action and reaction, by trial-and-error tactics in the competition among leaderships.

The advocates of the deprivation and access doctrines ridicule the riffraff theory, but they fail to provide alternative answers to central questions: Who are the leaders? Where do they come from? Why do certain people follow them at certain times? Why are certain tactics more prevalent at one time than at another? These questions must be answered quite apart from deprivation-access conditions. Why do people follow this leader rather than another, this tactic rather than that tactic, now rather than at some other time? These are the key questions that surround confrontation, revolution, and political violence.

Eric Hoffer says quite rightly that leaders "cannot conjure a movement out of the void" (cited in Leiden and Schmidt, 1968, p. 676). But discontent and dissatisfaction exist all the time, somewhere, in some form, in all individuals. The ripeness of conditions is not entirely determined by the degree or kind of discontent. It depends upon the rightness of bargaining conditions to endow certain kinds of tactics with efficacy in enhancing future bargaining power to achieve all kinds of values, many of which do not even exist for the political actors until opportunity and success whet the appetite. Underlying conditions are relevant to commitments and excitability, but they are not an adequate explanation or cause. Political tactics are learned through trial and error, action and reaction, and those which prove efficacious tend to be reinforced and imitated. They tend to confirm themselves and the legitimacy of the leaders who propose and execute them. Thus from the bargaining process itself do the norms of political behavior spring.

Social disorganization is a differential and relative factor in social groups, a question of role, maneuverability, options. Any society, however orderly the interests and purposes of the powerful, may be disorderly, demoralizing, and entropic for those who are powerless. My desk is orderly to me when it is littered with the papers of my work; to the maid, my desk is a shambles of disorganization unless everything is sorted according to size and tucked away out of sight. Access is always differential because it reflects structure; disorganization is always relative to the outcomes of specific bargaining engagements in which social groups yield to the order of others as a means of achieving or preserving other values.

The theory to be developed here gives a central place to the dynamics of social bargaining equations in which deprivation, access, structure, stress or release from stress, values in conflict, conflict management, and so on are related elements that respond to bargaining outcomes just as they provide the setting and conditions of bargaining. This theory has the advantage of permitting full integration of factors in a universal model that is of parallel significance at all levels of human action, from interpersonal to international.

Law is the clothes men wear
Anytime, anywhere,
Law is Good-morning and Good-night.

Others say, Law is our Fate;
Others say, Law is our State;
Others say, others say
Law is no more
Law is gone away.

And always the loud angry crowd
Very angry and very loud
Law is We,
And always the soft idiot softly Me.
                              Auden, 1945, p. 75

PROCESS AND POLITY

3

We Westerners tend to be blinded by words like rationality, reason, objectivity, truth, and to think of them as unique to our own values. This we have in common with untutored and primitive men who seek to control nature by word manipulation in prayers and incantations. Words are important because they carry an operational code about what reality is and what to do about it. To give a thing a right name is to imply the proper and prescribed reaction to it. Words imply a frame of reference based upon values shared by others.

Rationality is not a value. Technically, it is merely the structure of language—a set of rules governing a sequence of propositions based upon irreducible axioms, principles, and definitions. "Rational" merely means uniform, continuous, sequential, capable of being weighed or measured, following certain logical rules of language. The syllogism is the basic unit of rationality; through it anything can be "rationalized," that is, made to appear rationally sequential. Some entirely absurd descriptions of reality can be thoroughly rational even though we may quarrel with underlying assumptions and selection of relevant facts. There is no difference in rationality between a description of reality based upon demons and devils and one based upon impersonal physical forces. The difference lies in the choice of irreducible assumptions about reality, working hypotheses which are validated by their success in achieving values. Such conflicting perceptions of reality do coexist in societies and in individuals because there is a wide variety of values to be served.

In the political realm, where pluralistic value systems are common, the value-relative basis of rationality becomes evident. A *coherent* communication is rational whether you agree with its tendency or not. Although *reasoning* and *rational discourse* are interchangeable terms, the common tendency is to load them with other meanings; *rational* is transformed into reasonable, moderate, constructive, and amenable to resolution through negotiation, conciliation, and compromise. The difference between violent and nonviolent modes of conflict resolution is not a matter of rationality or reason, unless one equates these terms with his own preferences for moderation and abstract talk.

Any prescriptive syllogism is meaningless except in terms of the emotional force which is attached to the first principle. The infinite regress of syllogistic reasoning ends somewhere with a commitment of self. Such commitments cannot be explained or understood by reasoning alone. Efforts to adduce rational principles for explaining social and political change are futile unless one grapples with the often illogical (more correctly, "inarticulate" or "incoherent," "excited") intensity of self-commitment which marks social movements.

In political terms, one may define rationality, as does the economist, in terms of optimizing choices and rewards. Such a concept is value-neutral and can be mated to any given set of values. Obviously, this use of the word "rationality" has little to do with its use in formal logic. One can be completely rational, in the sense of maximizing ones' bargaining position, without relying on a web of logical symbols and verbal discourse. This is surely the case with animals, children, and inarticulate persons. Much that passes for rationality on the part of the articulate person is merely post hoc rationalization or part of the bargaining process itself (not necessarily the most important part).

It is not unusual for behavioral rationality (optimizing choices and rewards) to constitute a distinct and separate dimension quite apart from symbolic rationality (logical consistency). To achieve the latter, it is often necessary constantly to refine and qualify a verbal bargaining position in order to make it accord with the contradictions and reversals that are inherent in behavioral rationality under conditions of bargaining.

Reasoning, favored by lawyers, writers, and others who live by words, is not indispensable to the action-reaction patterns of behavior used as a means of maximizing self-evident values. In the context of bargaining, rationality is a synonym for pragmatic success: rational behavior is behavior that works; irrational behavior doesn't work. As students of political behavior, we must avoid the fallacy that "my values, which work for me, are rational; yours, *which do not work for me*, are irrational!" A distinction so obvious as this perhaps need not be stated, except that it tends to be blurred, in a self-serving and tendentious way, as part of the verbal dimension of social bargaining.

In real bargaining relationships, rationality is existential and universal. One may postulate a kind of thermodynamic law of human behavior. Drawing a comparison with the law of conservation of energy, we may assume that men seek to conserve energy and values. Keeping in mind the law of entropy (the tendency in nature toward disorder and energy decay), one may assume that social disorder and decay are constant threats which human energy and values must overcome. In any specific bargaining engagement, one party's order becomes another's entropy. All parties at all times seek to maximize the former and to manage and overcome whatever amount of the latter is forced upon them by particular bargaining outcomes.

The New Political Science

Political scientists have traditionally been interested in constitutional and legal forms, structures, and systems. With the rise of the behavioral sciences in the 1930s, the emphasis has shifted. New tools and approaches provided by the sister disciplines, and increased awareness that formal systems did not tell the whole story, have brought attention to underlying, often informal, processes and relationships. It is now generally recognized that formal systems are something of a fiction whose real content depends upon other kinds of factors than formal rules. Emphasis upon individual and group behavior has moved toward study of the dynamics of authority relationships and bargaining. Just as the sociologist has moved from thinking about culture as an abstract structure of values to thinking about culture as a set of behavior patterns and society as a structure of relationships, so political science has moved toward sociology. Authority and bargaining relationships, both formal and informal, are discovered to be the substratum of formal policy-making, legislation, law enforcement. In the behavioral sciences, the distinction between social and political has become so blurred that the concepts are almost, but not quite, interchangeable.

Empirical study focuses on "behavior units" which are seen as parts of a whole hierarchy of systems, including the composite of individual personality, membership in large and small groups, both formal and informal, clusters and coalitions of groups organized in different patterns for different purposes, and so on (see Boulding, 1962; Easton, 1965). At the heart of research interest and theory development is the role of informal structures in performing the functions of socializing, recruiting, articulating, aggregating, structuring, and communicating the boundaries of conflict and accommodation, values, and behavior among groups and individuals.

The uncritical notion that values determine behavior through an abstract intellectual process is a vestige of the old doctrine of free will and the mind-body duality. Contemporary psychological and sociological studies have tended to reverse the principle, assuming that behavior arises from experience, trial-and-error, bargaining relationships, action-reaction conditioning. It is then rationalized and generalized in terms of attitudes, preferences, verbal formulations, and so on, which in their abstract and subjective form we call "values." Psychologist B. F. Skinner has played a leading role in this reversal. Both individuals and groups adjust symbolic value systems constantly to make their parts consistent and compatible. The form and content of ideologies reflects such rationalized values. However, working independently of these values, behavior continues to react to fresh experience and to the rewards and punishments of the bargaining process, with appropriate reinterpretations of old value systems to give apparent continuity and consistency to behavior. From this point of view, for example, a landlord who is forced by open housing laws to rent apartments to members of minority groups will eventually tend to rationalize his behavior in terms of values, becoming a genuinely open-minded egalitarian in the process and taking great pride in his conversion. If this be true, then it should indeed be possible to "legislate morality"— provided that the real bargaining relations of the informal polity reinforce the new norm.

Values are explanations of social situations and standards of appropriate action designed to produce desired goals and successful management. As social gestalts or paradigms held in common by large groups, values reflect group experience and bargaining positions. Insofar as they limit or predispose behavior in new situations, they also tend to stabilize and structure existing relationships.

A high degree of order and predictability is essential for the conduct of human affairs and the achievement of universal high-priority human values (such as manipulating and controlling the physical environment for sustenance, comfort, and convenience). The options available for internal organization are infinite. Furthermore, whatever the system of order prevailing, it is always subject to stress arising from its own dynamics as well as those from the physical environment. The most important and most typically human quality is *generalized adaptability*. Ashley Montagu says that man differs from his evolutionary antecedents because "he moved from a dimension of limited capacity for learning into an increasing, enlarging zone of adaptation in which he became entirely dependent upon learning from the man-made part of the environment, culture, for his development as a functioning human being." Far from being "phylogenetically programmed," man's behavior is characterized by a supremely developed nonspecific capacity for learning. "He has to learn his human nature from the human environment, from the culture that humanizes him . . ." (Montagu, 1968, pp. 14–15).

Because human behavior appears to be dominated by learned responses within a largely man-made environment, the options for social order are at once infinite and changeable. Any given system is orderly only in relation to certain given human values. Slavery may be an orderly state of affairs for the slave owner but at the same time make personal order impossible for the slave. The natural and inevitable process of growth and change is one of conflict, that is, relative disorder. The definition of order for any given relationship of social groups tends to reflect the values, interests, and behavior of those who dominate the hierarchical structure of bargaining relationships.

The history of crime reflects the history of law, which in turn reflects the normative systems of prevailing power groups, that is, the social and economic conditions with which their emergence is identified and by which it is perpetuated. In the words of W. H. Auden: "Law is only crimes / Punished by places and by times . . ." (Auden, 1945, p. 75). Crimes against property reflect laws which make property a built-in power advantage for certain individuals and groups, laws which developed during the commercial and industrial revolutions. The social values which receive the protection of a criminal code are those treasured by the dominant interest groups (see Leighton, 1937). The values of dominant groups are modified by shifts in the locus of power brought about by the emergence of new groups. A process of social bargaining forces modification, accommodation, and even revolutionary changes in the hierarchies of power.

In the process of shifting, integrating, and reintegrating the formal and informal hierarchies there is a strain toward humanizing power and conserving both energy and values. Organized groups are essential to human survival, and hierarchy itself is essential to the practical functioning of group life. But there is no absolute arbiter to determine among the options of changing order available to social systems and concretely represented by the conflicts of individuals and groups. In the midst of uncertainty, there must be a process of choice and provisional consensus. This process, the unremitting struggle for influence and authority, whose tide at any given moment is fixed by the formal authority structures of government and economic decision-making, is properly called "politics."

All individuals and groups seek to impose their own order around them. When a set of norms form a framework for the deliberate achievement of human purposes, they become part of a social institution. This term refers to the established forms or conditions of procedure characteristic of group activity. In the course of doing something, the members of a society repeat actions often enough to cause a pattern to emerge and become recognized, institutionalized, and internalized as a self-enforced norm.

The boundaries of conflicting systems of order overlap, creating arenas of social entropy (relative disorder) and competition. One set of values may become hierarchically dominant over those of other men and groups. The formal institutions of state authority reinforce them through socialization, consensus, and, ultimately, a monopoly on legal violence. This enables dominant groups to determine the choices available to the lower orders of the hierarchy. They organize and manage social policy, resources, and the environment in such a way as to reflect their own values of order, which limits the choices that remain open to conflicting value systems in ordering their own proximate environments. If the whole multileveled and differentiated hierarchy retains legitimacy (that is, achieves values for at least those groups capable of challenging its authority), the social system will remain stable, its power and negative reinforcement mostly passive, and the processes of collaboration and accommodation relatively successful (see MacIver, 1947, p. 77). Such an integrated social order minimizes disruption, destruction, and potential schism.

Legitimacy and Legality

Legitimacy and legality of state or group authority are by no means synonomous. The procedural-structural aspect of the social order generally enjoys the broadest consensus of values. However, the substantive norms of social relationships, the matter of rights and duties, leadership and policies, carry no such broad agreement;

they are the common grist of interest-group politics. Legality is an attribute of sovereignty. It is an abstraction which confers the authority of the state upon the acts, records, elections, and so on of those who conduct the offices of state power, and upon the code of law which regulates behavior. Legality is the technicality of formal consistency and adequate authority.

Legitimacy, on the other hand, reflects the vitality of the underlying consensus which endows the state and its officers with whatever authority and power they actually possess, not by virtue of legality, but by the reality of the respect which the citizens pay to the institutions and behavior norms. Legitimacy is earned by the ability of those who conduct the power of the state to represent and reflect a broad consensus. This is the familiar doctrine enunciated in the Declaration of Independence. Legitimacy cannot be claimed or granted by mere technicality of law; it must be won by the success of state institutions in cultivating and meeting expectations, in mediating interests and aiding the process by which the values of individuals and groups are allocated in the making, enforcement, adjudication, and general observance of law. Not all law is legitimate in this sense, whether because it is unenforced, unenforceable, or responsive only to sporadic and arbitrary enforcement by this or that police chief, policeman, judge, or jury. Laws that were once legitimate may still retain legality after losing legitimacy.

The complex components of the informal polity which vest the formal institutional structure with legitimacy are indispensable to the working of the political and social systems. Law enforcement and court and correctional activities are particular aspects of the system of social control, and probably the least important ones. They will not work when the informal systems by which individual behavior is integrated into a social order break down or suffer the cleavages of internal warfare. A criminologist claims that imprisonment is less punitive than, and dependent upon, its informal effects: "Stigmatization of [the prisoner] and his family; economic effects on his dependents; the mortification process instigated by a status inferior to that of policemen, court functionaries and correctional personnel; and restriction of social and economic privileges . . ." (E. H. Johnson, 1964, p. 24). Hannah Arendt writes that "authority excludes the use of external means of coercion; where force is used, authority itself has failed. The authoritarian relation between the

one who commands and the one who obeys rests neither on common reason nor on the power of the one who commands; what they
have in common is the hierarchy itself, whose rightness and
legitimacy both recognize . . ." (Arendt, 1961, pp. 92–93).

Most of the controls that exist within the informal polity are not
perceived because they are right under our noses and taken for
granted. They function within the context of personality development and all the commonplace activities of daily life and human
relations. When they work well, they are overlooked or considered
to be simply "normal" or "just human nature." The newspapers do
not report the performances of good fathers, obedient children,
honest cashiers, and so on.

We become aware of the informal polity only when the fragile
web begins to tear, partly because of the sense of danger, the irre-
pressible demand for attention, the evangelical energy liberated in
those individuals who themselves are torn by the rough edges of the
cleavage.

Whatever the historical, logical, or illogical culmination of events
that unifies a population under central state sovereignty, the subjective aspect of its unity—its legitimacy—makes it a nation. The
objective aspects, territorial boundaries, the letter of the law, the
monopoly of legality and police power do not in themselves make
a nation; in fact, they may generate more violence than collaboration unless a nation is built in the minds and hearts of the people.
It is the consensus that supports the informal polity that constitutes
the nation. Those who occupy the offices of state power face each
day the continuing task of validating the legitimacy of the state by
the way they manage and shape the life of the nation. This must be
done because of and in spite of divided regional loyalties, economic
rivalry, ideological and religious conflict, cultural variety, and the
like

The tension of normal social life is alive with ambivalence, conflicting loyalties, and shifting alliances of convenience. Competition
and cooperation are by no means incompatible; they are poles of
a continuum in a working social order. All individuals and groups
are torn between conflicting interests and impulses and struggles for
leadership and influence. Hostility and cooperation are intertwined
in a complex maze whose day-to-day movements and adjustments
are never conclusive. Ambivalence is the nature of the bargaining

of various kinds. All of those many institutional leaders who refused to bargain with Martin Luther King in the 1950s needed him desperately in their attempts to contain the eruptions of black militancy in the 1960s, and they had to meet many of his terms.

The options, values, and gradations of reward and punishment in the bargaining equations of the informal polity cover the whole range of human relations. The exchange of values that influences behavior among members of a bowling team need not be fundamentally different from the exchanges between legislators compromising on the terms of a new law. The difference arises from the functional scale of each group, one (the legislators) incorporating the interests of vast numbers of individuals, formal institutions, and informal groups, the other (the bowlers) representing the affairs of the bowling club only. Both formal and informal relationships are structured hierarchically by such differences of scale and by their specialized and differentiated social functions. At every level of organization, whether formal or informal, persons act upon and react to all those who are capable of imposing sanctions (either positive or negative reinforcement) on them. Decision-makers highly placed in formal vantages of power must consider all those individuals and groups who will respond to their decisions either positively or negatively. Personal obligations, loyalties, and the inescapable pressure of organized interest groups constitute the parameters of executive decision-making in government and business. Abstract high principle and hypothetical decision-making are easy; but their application in terms that affect behavior and bargaining relationships are always hard. Real decision-making (as distinct from empty declarations or intentions) must modify relationships and behavior and therefore must be constantly attended, implemented, evaluated, and enforced. All up and down the line, those who are affected can impose their own negative sanctions and costs. Formal office-holding is never all-powerful. The informal polity cannot be ignored or obliterated.

The process of action-reaction among individuals and groups is the underlying concrete reality which constitutes learned behavior. Such learning tends to reinforce and stabilize attitudes, habits, and responses in like, similar, and transfer situations. When new situations prove such behavior to be inappropriate and frustrating, the characteristics of search behavior are unleashed in a process of trial-and-error, including regression (the return to older patterns), invention (behavior whose main relevance is its unproven effects), imitation (trying to achieve the predicted result of another's behavior pattern), repetition of inappropriate responses, despite untoward results, coupled with denial of their inappropriateness (hysteria), and so on. Any of such options may prove adaptive depending on the individual's real bargaining situation, that is, the effect it has upon the actions and reactions of others.

Even hysteria, compulsion, or psychosis may have secondary effects which constitute adaptive reinforcement, fixing the individual in behavior patterns which constitute "mental illness" in terms of some functional requirements of his life situation, while maintaining the sick individual's power to satisfy his needs for attention, food, and housing. Many mental health hospitals today aggravate problems of mental illness by institutionalizing patterns of dependence. Patients play toward doctors, nurses, and visitors, who generally play back. An exception, Synanon, presents a method for curing dope addiction by "cold turkey" withdrawal, denying the least bit of drugs, sympathy, or indulgence to the new member, no matter how much he may agonize, cry, wheedle, or maneuver. This method has proved much more successful than those based upon sympathetic psychiatrists, gradual withdrawal from drugs, and absence of a socializing control group to reinforce the will-to-health.

In short, it is only the concrete and objective bargaining situation that links the complex webs of interrelatedness among all individuals and groups, and maintains or modifies behavior and personality. General principles, ideologies, and ethical codes are meaningless except as they are reinforced by the bargaining outcomes of the behavior which they prescribe. Pious and homiletic attitudes, intentions, or motives are insufficient to explain the causes of behavior. Similarly, exhortations and preachments, like the technicalities of legality, are reiterated most intensely when they are used to promote conditions that have already changed, or in defense of attempts to prevent change.

The key to understanding political violence and projecting methods for its management must be found in the dynamics of bargaining relationships rather than in the chance issues of the conflict. German sociologist Ralf Dahrendorf provides a fertile insight: "... the violence of conflict relates rather to its manifestations than to its causes; it is a matter of the weapons that are chosen. ..." The causes of social tension and the programs of protest or reform vary independently from the tactics of bargaining and mechanisms of conflict resolution (Dahrendorf, 1959, pp. 211–12). Organized power groups with ample means of adjusting conflict rely, he suggests, upon inside and peaceable means of influence, while those outside that are seeking organization tend toward provocation and direct action.

Status is an important vantage point of bargaining. Behind every quarrel, hidden deep within the issues of every dispute, lies a fundamental *authority* issue. Though frequently unrelated to the specific quarrel, it often overrides and becomes in fact the main issue. The question of status or authority reflects the viability of bargaining positions for future issues and quarrels, either among the same parties or with other parties. This is what teen-age gang members refer to as "saving my rep," and what nations regard as "prestige." Every quarrel provides a model for settling other issues and predisposes outcomes which replicate the model without other costly tests of strength.

Once a quarrel is escalated to a fundamental test of authority and status, the high costs of such a test tend to enforce its outcome without another major challenge for a long time. It is not uncommon for individuals to force a test of strength on relatively unimportant or silly issues. This tends to limit and control the danger implicit in the dispute by focusing upon less sensitive and provocative questions. People remember major arguments with loved ones without recalling what the argument was about. Every symbolic element of procedure becomes a matter of intense bargaining as diplomats prepare the way for negotiations to end wars.

This is why status values (reflecting the rank of individuals and groups in the hierarchy of authority) constitute one of the most fundamental aspects of human aspirations. It is literally a matter of life and death in the sense that the higher the individual or group status, the greater the power to bargain and to organize life boundaries in accord with a principle of order, thereby reducing relative entropy and optimizing ability to manipulate and control the requirements of life and growth. In this sense, status values are not unlike the requirements of living space and territoriality for other members of the animal and vegetable kingdoms. Loss of ability to eliminate entropy and bring order to one's personal boundaries is the greatest source of personal despair, desperation, and death. Recent studies have found the rate of heart attacks and other physical disorders to be clearly related to the achievement or nonachievement of status values. Drastic status reversals are closely related to accident-proneness, suicide, and aggression.

Government, Law, and Informal Polity

All institutions, private and public, formal and informal, emerging, prevailing, and declining, are made up of individuals and groups of individuals who are using whatever power and assets they possess to bargain to maximize whatever values they hold and to protect and advance whatever prestige and influence they enjoy. The formal structures of policy, law, and administration are only a last resort and an ultimate standard of comparative advantage. Parties to disputes, including government agencies, do not go to court if they can get satisfactory adjustment or compliance by merely threatening to go to court, or by finding other ways of trading off values at their command in order to reach amicable settlements. The law provides the ultimate claim, the courts the ultimate forum, against the ad hoc structure of discretionary policies that brings the law to bear in the details of the bargaining process itself.

A healthy society manages its affairs and the changing balance of power among domestic interest groups with a fair degree of flexibility and equity. Events and real power relationships among interest groups, regional groups, occupational groups, and the like are elements in a dynamic flux undergoing constant change in response to gyrations of leadership, accidents of human and physical environment, priorities and problems set by new conditions. Such factors bring continuous pressure to bear upon various parts of the formal system. The norms of law represent a crystallization of forces at some moment in the past. The structural basis of representation and the terms of elective office tend also to remain intact even though the popular balance of forces and values may have been modified. To resist erratic change is an important aspect of the law function. Law forces insurgent values and groups to seek a broader consensus over a period of time that permits mellowing before a new abstract legal model is created and before the personnel in the citadels of representation are replaced.

In influencing the behavior and roles of the institutions of government, the bargaining equations of the informal polity are of vastly greater significance than is formal party organization. Public office is but a vantage point of bargaining, albeit one of the most important in a society whose tasks and functions require highly centralized authority as a means of concerting and regulating all the resources (both human and physical) of the nation-state. Policies, proposals for new laws, allocations of resources, budgeting, and the organization of new activities inhere at this level. But the informal polity continues to be the source of feedback, pressures for or against change, the means of maintaining and preserving efficacy and legitimacy, and, therefore, the authority of formal government and the regime.

Political parties are headquarters staffs charged with operating the election machinery and providing administrative services for coalitions of formal and informal interest groups that ebb and flow around such issues as require centralized policy-making. Coalitions collect around these bases of operation for the specific purpose of selecting candidates. In addition, control of the party organization is itself a great vantage point of bargaining (especially where election of its candidates is certain), because it provides power to determine coalition membership and to influence office-holders who require support for renomination and reelection. Most of the real power of party leaders depends upon the informal assets by which they maintain their organizations. The informal polity is working all the time, while parties tend to build their coalitions cyclically to meet the dates on the election calendar.

Political parties tend to deal in the abstractions of personalities, while the informal polity generates programs and policies in terms of interests. For those "political men" who are specialists in resolving group conflicts, who become mediators and brokers between contending interests, the perception of issues is always concrete and personal. The question of substance ("What is the problem and what should be done about it?") is subordinated to questions of personality ("Who is for and against?" "How will they react to what I do?"). Substantive issues blur with personality equations in the perception and rationalization both of problems and of programs. The latter are obviously the most real and unavoidable; the former are always abstract, ideological, and fundamentalty unproven. Any decision, policy, or program is always tentative and subject to trial-and-error proof. If one decision or program doesn't work, it can be modified or discarded for another. Since no one is omniscient or clairvoyant, the bargaining equations of personal relations must be primary in decision-making. Even the feedback and evaluation of decisions is transmuted by the political process into such concrete equations: "Who is for and who is against what?" and "What can they do to me?"

The informal polity represents the underlying process which encompasses all vantage points and bargaining relationships. There is genuine paradox concerning *representation* between the formal government and party structure and the informal polity. Problems of imperfect apportionment and the single-member district tend to impose artificial distortions upon the values and interests, comparative numbers, and bargaining capabilities of formal and informal groups. The "one-man, one-vote" formula, even if perfectly realized, provides a less responsive and sensitive kind of representativeness than is provided by self-appointed pressure groups that bring to bear upon government and party officials whatever resources they possess. The degree of organization of groups, the intensity of commitment of their members, the level of cost-risk which they are willing to impose upon themselves and others—such factors represent the real balance of forces in the nation, a balance that is often quite different from the statistical fiction that all men and all groups are equally involved in any particular public interest.

Political accountability does not inhere in party structure or the apparatus of formal representation. Political accountability operates largely through complex networks of action and reaction of individuals and groups with real interests at stake and real capabilities for bargaining. They act and react upon each other and upon those who occupy formal vantage points in structures of government. The choice of tactics for bargaining and influence is largely a matter of differential access. When influence upon government is sought, there is little difference between the soft word spoken to the President on the golf course by his industrialist friend, and the harsh words echoing shrilly from a demonstration by poor people at the Lincoln Memorial.

The legal system is more than a code of rules; it is a complex organism that includes the making, interpretation, implementation, and enforcement of law in terms of public policy. The legal code in itself is merely an abstract model of accepted social relations. It is strangely and tacitly amended, stretched, distorted, and sometimes ignored in the complicated bargaining and exchange of values that constitute the real substratum of national life, the informal polity. The entire structure constitutes a process of which formal law is only a part. Because of the way they are generated and enforced, legal institutions at any given moment generally reflect the balance of social power among organized groups. The legal code, that is, the Law, serves peaceful political change by emphasizing underlying unity, stability, continuity, equity, and logical consistency of the state.

However, the inertial lag built into the legal system can bring change to a total stop. Some responsiveness to informal change is necessary; the past must be superseded as well as conserved. Thus the legal system in all its elaborate byways is immersed in policy and politics which, taken together, constitute the social process. All who hold office in the institutions of legislation, execution, enforcement, and judicial settlement and interpretation are involved in a process of bargaining among themselves and outside individuals and interest groups. All to some degree bend the austere logic of the legal code to maintain certain values or to yield to new claims by insurgent interest groups. Whether explicitly promulgated in courts, regulatory agencies, the Department of Justice, and police departments, or quietly arranged by gentlemen's agreement between key men, multitiered policy choices are continuously changing the abstract norms of law, giving it many different meanings in many different situations and bargaining engagements. The legal system is loaded with interpretations, exceptions, favors, and deliberate blind spots.

A structure of policy choice, most of it ethical and proper, pervades the operations of the legal system; In effect this structure of choice embodies experimental or instant lawmaking which may later be codified or countermanded by the formal lawmaking process. The President and the whole administration down to the most obscure petty bureaucrat, the courts and their administrators, the cadres of lawyers (for whom the legal system is less an automatic set of norms and sanctions than a threat used to force out-of-court settlement in the majority of suits), the hoards of inspectors, tax collectors, contract officers, state attorneys general, county state's attorneys, sheriffs, police chiefs, and even individual policemen— all within the purview of their own authority may pursue policies which amend the legal process toward greater or lesser severity and even, in some cases, toward complete revocation of statute law, by soft or selective enforcement, or by nonenforcement. This structure of formal and informal policy built into the legal system reflects the ongoing, day-to-day process of interest-group bargaining and power. Individuals and groups with considerable bargaining power enjoy privileges not only embodied in law but further augmented by these informal policy aspects of the legal process.

To retain legitimacy and to fulfill its conserving function, the law must reflect and coordinate the multitudinous policies by which it is changed in individual instances so that in the long term it may more closely approximate the balance of forces within the state and the relation of these forces to the priorities and problems of national life. Yet the very stability of the legal system makes it vulnerable to an ill-use that may undermine its legitimacy and cause social disruption. Powerful groups of the status quo may use legality and the police to maintain their privileges and social norms that no longer reflect the real bargaining relations between groups. This is especially likely when their own legitimate social assets are weakening and when their interests are undergoing serious challenge.

Ralph Waldo Emerson long ago said that a good citizen should not be too obedient to law, that men came before laws and will be here after laws are in limbo

Clarence Darrow said, "Nothing is so loved by tyrants as obedient subjects. Nothing so soon destroys freedom as cowardly and servile acquiescence. Men will never have any more liberty than they demand and are ready to fight to take and preserve" (Darrow, 1932, p. 297). Blackstone, too, a great respecter of law, noted that no man who bases his conduct solely on the law is either honest or good.

The content of the law at any given time always advantages some and disadvantages others. One of the various games of life, the making of the law is never an impartial process; in an imperfect society the legal process is necessarily part of the stakes of the game. Whoever is advantaged by the law in his bargaining relationships with others will want to maintain what is legal; he will assert the automatic enforceability of "the letter of the law," and he may seek to buttress old laws by new ones which narrow or foreclose the gambits of future discretion.

A good example of the interaction of law and the informal polity can be seen in the recent history of so-called stop-and-frisk laws. Since time immemorial it has been the practice of policemen to stop and frisk (without authority, but with impunity) members of minority groups, the young, the poor, and the helpless. The sudden interest in laws to authorize such activity rises from the fact that the practice is no longer feasible. Members of the affected groups have sought judicial remedies for illegal stopping and frisking. More important, residents of the black ghetto are now achieving self-consciousness and organization, and they are no longer helpless. Police attempts to honor the ancient practice of stopping and frisking lone Negroes now create an angry crowd. Bystanders intervene to prevent both frisking and arrest. Several major riots have been sparked by this kind of incident. In effect, the violent reaction of large numbers of Negroes has changed the bargaining equation.

Police officials and some members of the white community claim that effective law enforcement requires that the power of the government be brought to bear to offset the informal but effective power of an alert and concerted black community. So stop-and-frisk laws are passed by legislators and even upheld by the Supreme Court. The police continue to stop and frisk the helpless. But, strangely enough, the law fails to offset the new capability of the black community to deter its enforcement—so the police no longer stop and frisk Negroes unless they find one all alone on the street. And policemen are encouraged to show great restraint even in this, since some lone blacks will resist, forcing the police to escalate the use of force. The Negro injured, shot, or arrested and charged with "disturbing the peace" or with being a "suspicious person" may arouse hordes of riotous blacks tomorrow.

The result is that stopping and frisking of blacks is being done less now, with an authorizing law on the books, than it was before it was legalized. Instead, the police use the law to continue the practice on teenagers, college students, and other groups who remain helpless, just as they were prior to the law's enactment.

The nation's tax structure tends to reflect the relative advantages and power of social groups. Garnishment laws advantage the "schlock" merchants who sell on credit, while they drastically disadvantage the poor and the legally unassisted. Anatole France made the point succinctly when, in *Battle of the Angels*, he saluted "the majestic equality of the law" which "punishes rich and poor alike for sleeping under bridges or stealing loaves of bread." There is danger in the exploitation of the conserving elements of the legal system by narrow interest groups that seek either to maintain advantages or to achieve new advantages which do not reflect their real social and political bargaining power. The power of the state is used to make and enforce ever more detailed laws which deny policy options and discretion to administrators, interpreters, and enforcers. In the name of an abstract legal doctrine, such a trend jeopardizes the legitimacy of the legal process itself. This process is a more fundamental basis of social consensus than the legal code of the moment; its legitimacy is the best guarantee of continued peaceful social change. When we speak of "justice," "charity," and "mercy" as being of higher value than "law and order," we are in effect recognizing the reality of the informal polity and the need to maintain the ultimate legitimacy of the legal process.

To maintain legality at the expense of legitimacy can be more disruptive of social tranquillity than to challenge legality in order to discover or create legitimacy. The doctrine that every good citizen obeys every law is an ideology of the status quo. Obviously, nobody really believes or observes it, even those with a strong vested interest in the status quo—except in regard to those laws that serve their interests. The legal code is an abstract normative model. If it gets too much out of kilter with political reality, or if narrow interest groups use it as a wall against social change, then disadvantaged individuals and interest groups may break the law. They may do it out of convenience, and covertly, as all of us break some laws. They may do it out of desperation and despair, covertly if possible. They may do it in spontaneous defiance, openly and with vehemence, flinging their inchoate rage into a terrible act against a policeman or a citizen who seems for a moment to symbolize the cause of their disadvantage. They may do it openly, deliberately, and tactically in order to bring self-consciousness and organization to the ranks of all who are disadvantaged, to create a new interest group capable of asserting social power, thereby bringing about social and legal change. They may do it as a method of testing the consensus and legitimacy behind the advantages of certain power groups. To the disadvantaged, all these motives are clearly related, even if they are not in the minds of the lawbreakers.

In sum, many of the slippery qualities of the legal system embody an adjustment to the realities of interest group politics, the changing nature of the domestic balance of power, and the nature and priorities of social problems and solutions. The informal polity provides the salient facts, which the law can only ratify, and to which the law ultimately conforms, either explicitly or otherwise. Private violence and threat, like other kinds of social bargaining power, are part of the underlying social process. Laws, court decisions, and government policies that are not supported by the informal polity are seldom effective. Just as black demonstrations in the South forced the enactment of major civil-rights laws, riots in the North may prove necessary to create a sense of urgency for real implementation of these laws. This becomes possible only when other social groups decide it is better, after all, to share their jobs, public services, and neighborhoods with new groups than to continue a process of terror and counterterror.

In the final analysis, the rules maintained by the bargaining relationships of both formal and informal polities enforce the actual normative systems of behavior. A norm is actual and effective only when its neglect or infraction is met by the application of bargaining sanctions by those individuals and groups who possess the interest and the capability to maintain the norm (Bohannan, 1967, p. 187).

Formalizing Consensus

The existence of legal codes and institutions raises only slight impediments to the pluralistic bargaining relationships of the social process. The formal structural and procedural elements of the law (about which there is the largest and most stable consensus) tend, insofar as they retain legitimacy, merely to regulate and structure the bargaining relationships without necessarily affecting the bargaining. In many respects they protect the bargaining ability of some who are otherwise weak in such assets as private organization, leadership, finances, property, personal relationships, skills, and good looks. In the normal course of political change, a matter rises to the level of legislative debate and consideration when the existing code no longer provides an adequate basis for private bargaining claims or for third party adjudication. That is, it is no longer acceptable to those who have the power to challenge it. Proposals of new laws, repeals, amendments, appropriations for enforcement, and the appointment of judges *formalize the process of social consensus building*. Lawmaking summons to the public forum all the interested social groups. It brings into being a ritual display of the values and resources of power and influence of the whole community. It forces the complex informal structure of group power and leadership into a formal interplay.

Such tests of strength, and the accommodations that emerge from them, are in many ways more durable and significant than the elections of congressmen and presidents, processes which are similar in effect because they determine comparative representation in much the same manner. But there is a difference. The alignments and coalitions of slate-making, balanced tickets, endorsement, and election do not in themselves create substantive norms of social behavior. Representation is significant but rarely determining. Most of the elected legislators assess and respond to the specific issues of a given bill in terms of the new legal norm's consequences for the social bargaining situations it will modify. The reason for this independence of judgment is simply that such considerations reflect the social consequences and costs that private groups can impose, and such considerations shape the coalitions of interest groups for the next election.

In legislative debate, alignments and coalitions emerge as interest groups trade off marginal values in order to enhance their strength in regard to values that are more central and significant and com-- mand broader support. Every individual and group with an interest, active or passive, in the regulation of a particular kind of behavior is likely to be drawn into some level of pressure activity at the fringes of the solons' pit. The process of changing a word or inserting a comma becomes a form of symbolic maneuver which aims at consolidating forces, mediating demands, assessing bargaining terms and positions. The problems of language are not only a technical matter. More important, they are symbolic surrogates for the larger, more sensitive, and more divisive issues; and they present a test of strength for all the parties in the society who play a role not only in spelling out the new law but also in spelling out the changed equation of social relations and the new norms of individual and group behavior, many of them informal, which are much broader and more far-reaching than the legal fictions. What must emerge is not merely a law but changes of attitude and accommodation of conflicting interests which will give the law and the lawmaker legitimacy and the new behavior practical support and efficacy.

The legislators themselves (at least the most effective ones), though they may represent certain interest groups, are forced to become brokers and mediators far beyond the original loyalties of their nomination and election. Their dedication tends to move toward the new consensus, toward the emerging social system whose norms of behavior and contrived process of bargaining-accommodation have, in effect, been created by the charade of making a law. Through this process is performed the indispensable service of keeping the authority of law intact; of enabling the nation to retain a workable legitimacy; of supplying new norms of political socialization, however provisional, when they are needed; and of inducing a general efficacy of social control which is largely capable of policing itself through the formal and informal, private and public, individual and group bargaining processes, and which will win the general support of the community in the few instances where it must be policed and enforced by the state.

Political leadership has a responsibility and a motive to assess the informal power behind the conflicting demands of social groups and to find a basis of accommodation in terms of cost and risk. In doing this, political leaders must adjust their own and their followers' values to make the accommodation feasible, or face the dangers of direct action and escalated violence and counterviolence. When a community drifts toward alienation and violence, leaders of the establishment cannot evade the responsibility of adjusting majority values in order to moderate minority needs. In such a situation a popular referendum may widen the cleavages and intensify the danger. Lawmaking moves the confrontation into a manageable dialogue which changes the norms and attitudes of the whole society. The law may be viewed as the scar tissue of the body politic. Those laws are most tough and resilient whose making involved the most representative bargaining process and whose prescribed behavior norms and structural relationships permit continued flexibility, bargaining, and generally fair and acceptable accommodations between social groups.

Social catharsis helps to maintain the continuity and stability of the society in the face of the inevitable and frequently insoluble tensions that exist at all times in all human groups. Not all problems can be solved, and conflict is omnipresent. The more people have in common, the more intensely they argue about less important things. The more closely men collaborate, the more things they find to differ about. Tension is as universal and inescapable as the search for tranquillity and order. The means of transmuting and releasing tension, of converting persistent and chronic elements of conflict into constructive forms, are not without value in controlling potential disruptions and maintaining general continuity. This is an important factor for insulating the legitimacy of the legal system. In the face of inevitable judicial and legislative corruption, miscarriages of justice, bad policies and bad laws, personal and group antagonisms that shift because of social cleavages but also because of personal failures, aging, germs, and accidents—in the face of all this there is a human need to avoid too much reality. A great deal of real accommodation of conflict occurs under a slight blur of ambiguity which permits graceful retreats, threats and promises understood without being spoken, emphasis on common interests, however marginal, rather than on divisive facts, however massive.

The legal process may be viewed as a set of unifying myths and institutions which serve a wide range of uses, including that of a theater-in-the-round, a circumambient divertimento that dramatizes and gives meaning to our lives, even if it lies a little. In the legislative theater, the actors more or less consciously recognize their roles and cultivate contrivance, artfulness, dramatization, plot, and story. They act as if their function, far from being limited to lawmaking, includes the venting of the collective subconscious of the nation. Senator Dirksen knows that most of the issues thrown at the Congress are not soluble there and may be insoluble altogether; in the meantime, the healing balm of time must be purchased by artful delays and dodges. The doctor's bedside manner constitutes more than half of his healing art and has little to do with medical knowledge. The "tale told by an idiot" may be an important tale which serves to ease our deeper recognition that new conflict will replace old and many old conflicts will remain; that it may be more important to find ways to live with unresolved conflict than to seek to force a consensual solution for every issue that arises with each day's grief.

The legal structures and rules provide norms where other normative systems of behavior do not exist or lack sufficient uniformity and universality. There is a tendency to underestimate man's anxiety to obey, to follow a rule. In a more or less stable society most people get trained by life to do adequately the things that are required of them. Most people are disposed to repeat habitual actions which, even if not noticeably successful in achieving values, at least are not noticeably unsuccessful either, and are generally approved by the community. In this sense, the legal system is an explicit and learned pattern of behavior concerning certain types of conflict or actions that affect others. It is often better to have a rule, even a poor rule, than to have no rule at all or divergent rules.

By and large, most people, on most issues, are not part of an active minority deeply involved in a particular value which is in the throes of social dialogue. On most issues they will embrace the normative fashion, wherever it comes from. This is functional for society because it ensures that the active minorities who become the *publics* of particular issues may assert and build their influence and eventually change the norm of law without at the same time discrediting the stability of the law or upsetting the general tendency of most people most of the time to adhere to most laws.

Reprisal: Push me, and I'll push you back!

Escalation: Push me, and I'll break your head!

ESCALATION AND REINTEGRATION

4

All bargaining contains an inevitable component of negative and destructive escalation. It is useful to define bargaining as a process of adjusting conflict through threatened or actual escalation and counterescalation—an equation of sliding scales whose points of respite and tentative balance (agreement or accommodation) result from a mutual testing (whether symbolic or actual) of mutual capabilities and cost-risk constraints. In each transaction, the parties have many values to exchange, both positive and negative, the most extreme point being complete withdrawal or exclusion from future bargaining and collaboration. For the group, this extreme is the ultimate sanction against disloyalty; for the individual, it is an act of rejecting the legitimacy of the group. It is also the point at which bargaining relationships are converted to separation, or to confrontation, tests of strength, physical violence, and open warfare.

This denouement is usually labeled a "breakdown of bargaining." That is not entirely accurate. Confrontation, warfare, and personal violence between related individuals do not exclude a continuation of the bargaining process. In its early stages, a test of strength and will tends to be conducted symbolically by threat, by withdrawal, or by limited and token displays of force. When symbolic and token displays of force are despised by their target, or elicit counterescalation, then a higher magnitude of risk-cost is imposed upon all the parties.

The avenue back to constructive bargaining grows more and more blocked. It is at this point that lovers kill the thing they love, and college presidents call in the gendarmes, while students seek ever more provocative forms of retaliation. This explains why thirty-eight percent of all homicides are committed within the family, why another forty percent occur among close friends, why more children are killed by abusive parents than die from leukemia, cystic fibrosis, and muscular dystrophy combined. The lone assassin generally is found to be strongly attached to his victim, having gone through periods of great love and admiration and frequently identifying with him even after a sense of rejection has led the assassin to threaten or attempt an act of mad and fantastic revenge, punishment, retaliation, and, in his view, purification.

The opposite of war is not peace, the opposite of love is not hate, the opposite of collaboration is not harassment. In terms of bargaining relationships; each of these dichotomous pairs is at the same end of the scale of mutual involvement and relatedness; at the opposite end of the scale lie separation, indifference, exclusion, and rejection. Failure to comprehend this model of a bargaining continuum contributes to the description of extreme forms of behavior as "meaningless," and prevents us from understanding and responding appropriately when bargaining engagements drift toward the breaking point. However, failure to assess correctly the role of bargaining is a universal and probably inevitable habit. Unfortunately, but inherently, the very failure of intelligence (a failure which raises the risks) may confer tactical advantages in a bargaining situation.

Thoughtful and far-seeing appreciation of the dynamics of escalated and counterescalated actions generally springs from or is interpreted as weakness and willingness to make concessions. Such a mood tends to legitimize the escalated actions of others. Thus intelligent assessment of danger may be read by one's antagonists as an incremental advantage which ensures the efficacy of further escalation. This is the fundamental paradox of the bargaining equation and a formidable challenge to hopes that mankind will find a way to avoid self-defeating wars and violent domestic and personal confrontations. Most of the time, men and groups grant concessions and reduce demands only in the face of grave dangers and disasters already enacted or immediately at hand. This fact accounts for the great melodramas and tragedies of human history, adding massively to the common woe and offering an ominous portent of the future. A scientist can only hope that understanding the dynamics of conflict will eliminate at least the most asinine and unnecessary denouements, facilitating assessments of cost-risk constraints in future bargaining outcomes well before the breaking point of violent confrontation.

Social change often pursues a logic that defies prediction and is logical only in retrospect. Whether union strikers attack scabs, sit in, or quietly picket cannot always be planned or controlled or carefully evaluated by union leadership. One shove of a woman picket by a plant manager or a policeman may suddenly focus years of accumulated grievances and unrelated suffering, forcing the leadership reluctantly to follow the followership or lose the technical role of leader. The political bargaining values of accidental violence and its ballooning aftermath are not calculable. In many situations the escalation toward illegality and violence does not have to be inspired or planned, but cannot always be controlled. Yet it becomes a part of the bargaining relationship and has influence on the assessment of options available to the bargaining parties.

Groups threatening or actually engaging in violence cannot be disregarded, even if they are typically small. Coser notes, "Given the psychic costs that are always involved in the use of violence, it is to be expected that only relatively small numbers of men will at any given time be ready to engage in a politics of violence. For only a few will the psychic gains of violence outweigh the costs. But the very fact that they are able to break with the habitual wont and use of the political game gives them a specific weight that is out of proportion to their sheer numbers" (Coser, 1967, p. 107). The very fact that options are limited tends to endow the desperation of such groups with political efficacy. The self-fulfilling prophecy of violence by other groups or by state authority may enlarge the power of their example, inducing others to protect and support the extremists and to adopt similar tactics.

Small minorities can bring about important concessions on the part of the majority after the minority has been forced into extreme actions of high cost to all. It is simply the way things happen. The notion that somebody somewhere really can manipulate events, can plan and conspire and control the outcome of complicated bargaining relationships full of imponderables, is naive. Events in conflict situations are something that happen. Sometimes no one wants them. They want themselves. They are like major wars, which sometimes come as a result of diplomatic confrontations that are in no way different from a long series of earlier events that atrophied the sense of risk-taking and urge of self-restraint.

No scientist can unravel the complex web of action and reaction on the part of all the people who are doing whatever they are doing in order to perfect and maintain their interests, to thrust and parry, to maintain bargaining power; often they do it at great risk and cost to themselves because to do otherwise is to lose all hope for the future. Since Niebuhr, there is less tendency to characterize social change as "progress." What is so frequently termed "progress" is a rationalization of the consensus and respite that come after danger, conflict, and confrontation. It is a rationalization of repairing and rejuggling coalitions and group loyalties as the next great spasm gathers strength in the womb of history.

We may (arbitrarily and for convenience) distinguish two general classes which blend and interpenetrate at all stages: bargaining and warfare. *Bargaining* includes all those uses which aim at modifying the behavior of others in order to induce some form of accommodation, including such objectives as deterrence, compulsion, measured and appropriate reprisal or retaliation, preemption, and provocation. On the other hand, *warfare* represents the breakdown of bargaining and a test of strength by the last resort of acts which aim at extermination, destruction, unconditional surrender.

In real life, absolute warfare is either rare or nonexistent. Rather, even confrontation is "a continuation of bargaining by other means" and not "engagement to final elimination of one of the parties." Under conditions of confrontation, all the forms of violence appropriate to bargaining continue but at a higher level of commitment, effort, cost, and risk. Mutual restraints against further escalation continue to be effective at each stage of intensified conflict. The dividing line between bargaining and warfare, like that between diplomacy and military operations, is the point at which symbolic display, threats and assessments of danger, and various restraints are discarded by one or both parties, opening the way to rapid and infinite escalation. The search for advantage moves from display and demonstration to tactics of maximum damage, destruction, and defense, in effect challenging and testing the ultimate viability of both parties.

In the words of Che Guevara:

War is always a struggle in which each contender tries to annihilate the other. Besides using force, they will have recourse to all possible tricks and stratagems in order to achieve the goal. Military strategy and tactics are a representation by analysis of the objectives of the groups and of the means of achieving these objectives. These means contemplate taking advantage of all the weak points of the enemy. The fighting action of each individual platoon in a large army in a war of positions will present the same characteristics as those of the guerrilla band. It uses secretiveness, treachery, and surprise; and when these are not present it is because vigilance on the other side prevents surprise (Guevara, 1968, p. 7).

When this point is reached, all chances of future bargaining and accommodation rest upon the ability of the parties to endure as organized groups. As confrontation edges into warfare, the real viability of the parties is increasingly pitted one against the other. As restraints fail and conflict is escalated by tactics of greater cost and risk, the parties mobilize all their resources in order to endure as independent bargaining units. Offense, attack, and destruction of the other party by every practical means become necessary extensions of defense and survival.[6] To the extent that the parties maintain themselves, they prove their legitimacy and thereby make it possible at some point to resume the process of bargaining.

The distinction between the two conditions—bargaining and warfare—is difficult to make unless it rests upon a formal and artificial declaration of the parties and is legally defined. Baron von Clausewitz makes the distinction that *diplomacy* is suspended at that point where symbolic communication by words ends and direct communication by deeds commences. The state of open hostilities may be *total* (aiming at overthrow of the adversary) or *limited* (seeking some conquests on his frontier) (Clausewitz, 1943, p. xxix). In intranational conflict, the legal formalities of violent confrontation are less well developed mainly because a primary function of the nation-state is to prevent the occasion for such internal conflict by facilitating nonviolent bargaining modes. Only when an insurrectionary group occupies and holds territory may it be accorded rights of belligerency.

In a critical confrontation, the elements of danger and opportunity for all parties cannot be separated. They are essential reciprocals of the bargaining process. Where there is no genuine fear of increased risk, the likelihood of escalation increases. On the other hand, the presence of real danger for all tends to enforce restraints and thereby to facilitate the movement of confrontation away from warfare and back to bargaining. Artificial danger, abstract danger, danger that is not demonstrated and therefore not credible, does not do the job. The danger must be clear and present, volatile and

---

[6] "A party that cannot be absorbed or destroyed as an independent source of decisions is said to be *unconditionally viable.* A party that can be absorbed or destroyed by another is *conditionally viable* if the party that has the power to destroy it refrains from exercising this power. The party that can absorb or destroy another is said to be the *dominant* party. Thus, a party that is conditionally viable survives only at the will of the dominant party. Perhaps two kinds of conditional viability should be distinguished. There are some situations in which it does not pay the dominant party to extinguish the other; this might be called *secure* conditional viability. There are other situations in which it would pay the dominant party to extinguish the other but in which the dominant party refrains through goodwill toward the dominated. This might be called *insecure* conditional viability" (Boulding, 1962, p. 58).

potentially unmanageable. Symbols, words, and aggressive display alone may have the opposite effect, justifying extreme measures of prevention and anticipation by those who exercise the legal monopoly of state violence.

Despite the wishful thinking of moderate men, there is no easy, safe, and sanitized method of testing the cost-risk constraints of a confrontation crisis. *The very nature of risk is uncertainty of outcome.* The way to salvation perforce lies through the Valley of the Shadow. Bargaining is ambiguous and ambivalent. Even a superior capability to inflict death and destruction is not absolute. To those willing to accept the costs, the adversary's power to inflict unlimited punishment has no efficacy to deter. Knowledge of the inevitability of backlash may help to dampen the escalation of frontlash tactics.

Intrinsic uncertainty and ambiguity touch every aspect of the bargaining equation. The stronger party fears the desperation of the weaker and must appease or anticipate it. Appeasement will be read as weakness and may backfire by encouraging and strengthening the challenger. On the other hand, the costs and risks of preventive action limit the use of power and lead to the necessary but difficult task which always confronts the powerful, the task of using carrot and stick simultaneously.

The "rational" goal (in the behavioral sense of maximizing assets and options) of the threat of violence is accommodation of interests, not provocation of actual violence. Similarily, the "rational" goal of actual violence is demonstration of the will and capability of action, establishing a measure of the credibility of future threats, not exhausting that capability in unlimited conflict.

By and large, all violence has a rational aspect for somebody, even if not for the perpetrator. All acts of violence can be put to rational use, whether they are directed against others or oneself. This is true because those who apply the threat of violence in order to achieve a social or political bargaining posture are reluctant to pay the costs or take the risks of an actual demonstration of that threat. Many incoherent acts of violence are exploited by insurgent elites as a means of improving their roles or imposing a larger part of their values upon a greater political system.

Violence and counterviolence, at least in initial stages, tend to be symbolic and to constitute, in both domestic and international situations, a demonstration of latent but clearly potential escalation. An aroused private group may thus control "force" and "forces" exactly as the state does. Similarly, it may claim and possess legitimacy in their use and in the values and behavior norms favored by the group, especially when the legitimacy of the state is already weak and divided. Individuals and groups, no less than nations, exploit the threat, either tacitly or openly, as an everyday matter, whether they do so purposively, futilely, deliberately, or desperately.

Push-Push, Push-Kill

Primitive legal systems are built on reprisal—"an eye for an eye, a tooth for a tooth"—that looks to self-help rather than formal third-party settlement by state authority. It is clear that even the existence of the state does not entirely remove informal systems of reprisal, retortion, or retaliation among individuals and groups.

On the most rudimentary level, social bargaining is simple physical action and reaction. "If you push me, I'll push you back. If you kick me, I'll kick you back." When all the parties are more or less equally viable, a certain equity and balance occurs in such simple reprisals, limiting the escalation of force and acting either as a rough substitute for internalized socialization or bringing about such socialization. Simple tit-for-tat reprisals maintain balance and equity in children's play groups and among grazing cattle. However, social groups are structured and differentiated by means of a natural process through both the inequalities of the energies and viability of their members and the requirements of organized group life.

The formula becomes, "If you push me once, I'll push you twice and harder." In time this pattern creates pecking orders and deference pyramids which constitute the hierarchical basis of social organization. The threat of escalation as a deterrent, made credible by actual escalation from time to time, constitutes a claim of dominance or a challenge to existing patterns of dominance.

Extremes of political behavior occur in mixed combinations, amplifying or dampening each other. Dominance patterns are complex and variegated. While the outcome of one transaction tends to set a model for other bargaining engagements between the same parties, the assets, interests, and cost-risk constraints vary among transactions. Consequently, degrees of dominance and even complete role reversals may coexist differentially among the parties in separate areas of behavior. Indeed, such differential dominance in itself can be a source of conflict when one of the parties challenges the established model in a new transaction.

This is the most rudimentary process of socialization. It creates attitudes, habits, and specialized varieties of *niche* or *role* behavior which tend to maintain a given hierarchy as a normative system: some people have the privilege of being pushier than others and thus can impose values and policies on the group. In a well socialized and stable system, just a few collisions reinforce and maintain the structure with a minimum of pushing and shoving. The resulting political hierarchy is functional for all the group members since, in addition to minimizing intragroup violence, it maintains adaptive and unified patterns of behavior for the whole group in its relations with other groups and with the physical environment.

Simple reprisal is the commonest form of bargaining. It tends to be stable when "the punishment fits the crime," and when the normative systems of behavior it maintains meet the requirements of the individuals and groups and match their capabilities for bargaining (see Bohannan, 1967, pp. 38-41).

Blood revenge was, and in some cases still is, a universal social form in Biblical Israel, in contemporary Alaska among certain isolated Eskimo tribes, throughout Africa, and in all the backward areas of the world, including those of the present-day United States. Sumner notes that the Eskimo had no civil organization outside the family and denied the legitimacy of white man's justice. The management of conflict depended upon reprisal, "the immediate coercion of wrongdoers by force. Hence death often results. Retaliation is the sacred duty of every kinsman" (Sumner, 1940, p. 422). In modern urban societies, there are similar groups. A Tex-Mex laborer in Gary steel mills, fired by a white supervisor, returns with a gun and kills him in the name of simple reprisal justice. Within his own social groups and in the eyes of his family, he would be less than a man to do otherwise.

The Hatfields and McCoys were fearless country boys in the mountains of Kentucky; while seeking to destroy each other, they observed the law of the hills and joined together to fight the revenuers. Injuring each other by aiding the feds would have been unanimously condemned by their neighbors, who would have withheld from them the aid and support necessary to continue the quarrel. If one reprehends a Jibaro Indian because he has killed an enemy, his answer is, "He has killed himself." His religion informs him that his brother's ghost will destroy his own family if one of its members does not avenge the blood of a murdered father, brother, or son (Bohannan, 1967, pp. 310–11).

Margaret Hasluck studied the informal polity of Albania. She noted this pattern: when the family of a murdered man, in default of government action, took the punishment of the murderer into its own hands and killed him or one of his male relatives, the head of his family might admit that both sides were equal and make peace. On the other hand, while still admitting that both sides were equal, he might prefer to continue the feud by killing a second male from the avenging family; that done, a second life was forfeit on his side.

In this way the feud might rage backwards and forward for years or even generations, each family being in turn murderer and victim, hunter and hunted. "To take vengeance" was "to take the blood" (that is, of the man already killed, not of him who was to make atonement); the criminal was called "the bloodstained," and avenger and criminal thought of each other as the "enemy" (Hasluck, 1954, pp. 219–20).

Throughout the labyrinth of the informal polity simple reprisal, retortion, and retaliation go on as the common denominators of all viable relationships, with each action being met in kind. When the boss fails to say "Good morning," his secretary makes it a point to leave without saying "Good night." When her boyfriend dates another girl, the girl dates another boy, preferably his friend. When the husband criticizes his wife's coffee, she soon finds reason to complain of his cigarette ashes on the rug. Such simple reprisals represent a negative exchange of values and span the whole spectrum of behavior along with the more positive and ongoing exchange of values that operates concurrently and reciprocally.

Subcultures of Violence

When positive values are not available as a medium of exchange (either because one party lacks values to exchange or his offer of that value has already been rejected), the likelihood increases of a continuation of bargaining through purely negative values of limited or escalated physical action. Withdrawal, pushing, pulling, running away, and so on are among the negative options that all possess. Groups or individuals who have few of the many positive exchange values available in social life must make the best of what they have. They therefore become specialists in applying various kinds and degrees of negative values. This is the primary cause of the so-called subculture of violence among the young of all social groups and among disadvantaged minorities whose resources and behavior options are sharply circumscribed by poverty and exclusion from organized and legitimate activity. The culture of "push and push back" exists to some extent in all walks of life, but it becomes legitimate and normative in backward societies where frontier conditions and the absence of higher legitimate normative systems of behavior forces the use of the only values available, a large proportion of which are necessarily negative. Under these conditions, reprisal, retaliation, and retortion are the natural law and take the place of formal institutions provided by law and state. They may be viewed as a primitive kind of law and state which may under certain conditions be formalized.

Self-help, vendettas, clan and tribal murder chains (feuds)—all the common forms of low-grade warfare—become the daily means of life, the legitimate manner of conduct, the model for normative virtues, and the only means of working out relationships upon which a higher level of social integration and organized group life can be established. Norman Lewis notes that in Sicily the vendetta was the weapon readily available to the poor and otherwise defenseless members of a society where law did not exist and justice meant the baron's court and the baron's torture chamber.

Sicily—the America of the ancient world—has been a colony exploited by the use of slave labor, either openly or in a disguised form, for two thousand years. The Roman armies marched to the conquest of Gaul and Britain on bread made from corn grown by Sicilian slaves. When, with the fall of Rome, the Papacy took over the great Sicilian estates, it was the chain gangs of Sicilian peasant laborers that provided three-fourths of its wealth. Sicily was exploited by Norman, German, Frenchman, Aragonese, Spaniard, and finally the Bourbons, but nearly always from a distance. After the Germans there was no central government, no monarch, no court, no resident hierarchy (Lewis, 1964, p. 32).

We witness today in the new nations the paraphernalia of the modern state, with sovereign national institutions, constitutions, political parties, foreign industries, and Fulbright exchange students. Yet none of these have yet succeeded in integrating the fractured and dispersed tribal groups who constitute the legitimate hierarchies of social life. Low-grade (and sometimes high-grade) systems of reprisal warfare are the normal method of relating groups and individuals in areas where interests and activities collide or overlap. Even for the small minority of national leaders and professionals who live in the pseudo-European towns left by departing colonials, formal institutions are virtually ignored—while the immemorial informal systems of reprisal justice, retribution, payoff corruption, and the settlement of disputes by ancient tribal elders and medicine men are the underlying reality.

Even in highly integrated and advanced societies however, there are backwaters and enclaves where groups denied admission to formal justice must look to their own barrios for social integration by the universally available and often raw means. Along with intergroup and personal reprisal, they keep alive such traditions as still serve to soften violence. But in terms of the state and established formal institutions they are outcasts and outlaws. They look upon these as hostile external forces and adopt an attitude of warfare and counterexploitation. Jobs, welfare, and crime alike assume the aspect of predatory raiding of an enemy camp. The United States, like

Europe with its gypsies, has many levels of nonintegrated or only nominally integrated groups, including immigrants and migrants (both white and black) in large urban areas, the young of all cultural and racial backgrounds (now, because of the World War II birth rate, a majority of the population), blacks, Puerto Ricans, and so forth.

In addition to the historically disadvantaged, another group suffers the same condition for other reasons: those involved for gain in criminal activity, such as vice, narcotics, or betting, represent values and needs that are denied legitimacy by the formal institutions of state authority while they have considerable legitimacy for large numbers of the population. Since anything that is available and desired will be sold and used, vast industries and social activities develop "outside the law," that is, without the benefit of normative reinforcement and adjustment through the centralized authority systems of the state, sometimes in defiance of attempts to enforce the formal code. Such activity therefore tends to be regulated through primitive reprisal justice. When such informal procedures lead to excessive cost-risk, as for example in the gang wars of early prohibition, informal institutions of integration emerge at higher levels—for example, in the case of organized crime, syndicates like Cosa Nostra and national Apalachan-type councils for mediating conflict, enforcing and adjudicating rules of jurisdiction, rights, and privileges, and limiting the risks of open warfare that surround all competitive activities, leadership succession, changes in functions, and norms of organization.

In their book, *Murder, Inc.,* two crime reporters noted the process:

"One guy gets hit, and his troop hits the outfit that did it," the protagonist went on. Reprisal in mob murder always cost valuable manpower. But more: it exposed the underworld's most vulnerable spot—it brought heat from the Law. In the end, it helped no gang, for good men were being lost continually. Why not an organization, then, which could eliminate this weakness, simply by dealing with such matters to the interests of all? (Turkus and Feder, 1951, p. 98).

So, in the 1930s, the syndicate was born. The gang lords agreed on a board of directors that would include all the mob leaders, each with equal power. Each boss remained czar in his own territory, his rackets unmolested, his local authority unchallenged. No one— local or imported—could be killed in his territory without his approval. He would have the right to do the job himself or permit an outsider to come in—but only at his invitation. In fact, no lawlessness on an organized scale could take place in his domain without his sanction and entire consent, unless he was overruled by the board of governors.

Every mob leader now had behind him not just his own hoods, but a powerful amalgamation of all mobs. Every gang chieftain was guaranteed against being interfered with in his own area—and against being killed by a rival mobster. . . .
Soon, the criminal bands from beyond the East saw the strength in the union. The Brooklyn stool pigeons told us a second meeting was called in Kansas City, to hear from the Western executives. The Capone crowd from Chicago and the Kansas City mob liked the idea. Reports came from Cleveland and Detroit that the Mayfield Gang and the Purple Mob wanted in. Boston and Miami, New Orleans and Baltimore, St. Paul and St. Louis —all flocked to the confederacy of crime, until it was nation-wide (Turkus and Feder, 1951, p. 99).

The indiscriminate toll of gangsters lost through mob rivalries came to an abrupt end almost immediately!
The mode of governance which ensued was studied by the Senate crime committee in 1963. In all the criminal "families," important matters go through channels. At the last stage, the problem comes to one man—the buffer—and he takes it to the overlord. This procedure is strictly followed, but occasionally a low-level superior is permitted to speak to the boss on business. This is unusual, and requires following a set method. The member concerned must obtain permission from his immediate boss. This request then goes through channels to the buffer, who presents it to the head. All this communication is done in person. "Such a request is not honored except under unusual and urgent circumstances, or when it comes from an old friend." When a request is granted, the buffer picks up both the petitioner and his immediate superior, and brings them to a place previously selected as convenient and acceptable to the overlord.

The meeting is formal. The matter is discussed, the petition is made, and, in due time, a decision is rendered and handed down to the petitioner. This concludes the matter. These "appointments" are very infrequent, occur within families only, and differ from a "sitdown."

A sitdown develops when gangland peace is threatened by a dispute between members of the subsociety. At one time, force—frequent and ruthless—was the ultimate pacifier. According to the chiefs of these notorious clans, however, when open violence is used "the only winners are the cops." When an issue comes up, the syndicate's lesser leaders arrange to sit down and thrash it out. In most cases the issue can be resolved at this level. If necessary, it can go higher. On occasion, when the dispute reaches a higher level, the disputants find out that they are members of the same "family." Sometimes the quarrel must finally be referred to the highest authority, the heads of the families. Arrangements are made to meet, and the heads sit down and talk the matter out. Their decision is final. "The sitdown, really a peace conference, has eliminated clashes between established houses."

All disciplining of members of these tribes, including their murder, is done within the same house or family, by its own members. Thus, if a family member has violated the rules or refuses to abide by a superior's decision, he must be punished. This punishment varies from a warning through cutting him out of some lucrative endeavor to the ultimate—murder. Keeping the killing within the family eliminates the development of vendettas, makes it easy to perform the task, and paves the way for the disappearance.

Sometimes a sitdown decides murder is the only solution to the problem discussed. The homicide is assigned to the mob to which the victim belongs. Within a short time, the man disappears. These obliterations are carried out by Judases, "friends"—possibly actual blood relatives—completely trusted by the victim. The victim shows no fear, no change from routine, before his disappearance.

"You gotta get permission." The first time a newcomer to a family is told this, he is very surprised. He finds he must obtain permission to enter any illegal enterprise, commit a stickup or burglary, dispose of stolen property, or even borrow from a shylock.

The explanation given is that only undertakings in keeping with family policy will be allowed. As long as permission is obtained, the family will help with lawyers, bail bondsmen, and so on, if anything goes wrong. This is a practical consideration. Then, from a viewpoint of public relations, no crimes which may cause a great public outcry are desired (see United States Congress, Senate Committee on Government Operations, 1963, pp. 68–69).

In effect, the community of organized crime possesses real legitimacy and resources parallel to those of respectable society. It develops all the apparatus for policy-making and conflict management which characterizes the larger society in whose ranks its members mingle freely, obtain recognition and status, and in many cases belong. Such acquired legitimacy is a far more powerful force of real social bargaining than the abstract and hypocritical legality of ethics and morals. In the same manner, informal institutions among the young and the poor sometimes acquire solidity and eventual respectability as the wheel of generations and social evolution turns. All groups that develop new activities and values whose informal legitimacy endures, including, for example, religious sects and technological innovators, suffer early exclusion from the established order. In their beginning stages, many new activities, values, forms of organization and behavior develop their own systems of group integration, falling back upon patterns of reprisal and self-help among themselves and in their relations to the economic and police power of the formal system. This can be clearly seen in the early history of mining, shipping, and industrial labor, for example.

Reprisal justice among the excluded recognizes both honor and duty in acts of vengeance and personal punishment. In the words of a Sicilian peasant, "Say that I have some animals and that one day they are stolen; well, naturally, if I've got the courage I'll go and kill the robber. . . . And if I haven't, then I'm stuck like a vine in bad earth, condemned to wither; in other words, I'm lost" (Dolci, 1964, p. 53). Walter B. Miller, Marvin E. Wolfgang, Albert K. Cohen, Richard A. Cloward, and Lloyd E. Ohlin, among other sociologists, have extensively analyzed the "subculture of violence." They have found a strong sense of legitimacy behind the quick resort to physical combat as a class-based problem-solving mechanism. Lower-class parents are more likely to use physical punishment than are middle-class parents, thereby inculcating in the young a normative pattern which serves many useful purposes for both young and old.

A number of demographic studies of murder show it to be related to geographical locale and socioeconomic group. Robert Bensing and Oliver Schroeder show that murder rates vary inversely with such factors as median family income, median number of years of schooling, and median occupational status of the residents of a neighborhood. On the other hand, there is a direct relationship between homicide and the rate of public welfare, overcrowding, and low median age. (Bensing and Schroeder, 1960).

On the other hand, the middle-class bargaining spectrum tends to avoid violence, running instead through withdrawal and withholding of positive values (reduced allowance, denial of use of the car, etc.), including the self (staying away from home, moving out, coming in late). Escalated to the next stage, bargaining is likely to be a resort to settlement by ministers and psychiatrists. Beyond that, there are the courts, with the possibilities of separation and divorce for husbands and wives, and other such solutions. At all points of the continuum, physical assault or suicide is logically present as a vague or explicit threat, tending to enforce unwritten laws about what options of thrust and counterthrust are appropriate at each point of conflict. Assault and suicide are likely to be carried out only when the unwritten rules are violated or there is suspicion of secret violation, especially when such an act threatens the viability of future bargaining for one of the partners. Even here among the great middle classes, statistics demonstrate that individuals who are highly integrated in social groups are more likely to injure or kill themselves than the other party. As we have seen, the opposite is true for the poor and the young.

The ability to command positive values tends to soften the content and methods of interpersonal bargaining. This is reflected and rationalized into a value preference which abhors violence entirely. Parents and teachers intervene to check the "push and push back" pattern universal among children. Instead, the approved form is to resolve conflict by redistributing positive values such as attention, material things, candy. One prevailing pattern of negative reprisal is, "Push me, and I'll talk you to death." The lecture becomes a pseudo-punishment which the middle-class young soon learn to practice on each other.

Values which renounce all forms of personal violence, including self-defense, are frequently counterproductive. A child who is taught not to fight back must either surrender to a bully or forgo his company (and the opportunity to socialize him). The child who defends himself, even though he is smaller and runs some risk of injury, will generally force the bully to learn other ways of conflict resolution and play. He can associate with the bully on more acceptable terms and may be spared future thrashings. The weaker and smaller child need not be taught pacifism as an instrument for pacifying those who are stronger and larger than he; it sometimes has the opposite effect, and in any case, he will learn this through the natural process of action and reaction. The parent does the child a disservice in urging him to generalize this tactic even to such provocations as require a response in kind.

Violence and Reintegration

Bargaining by reprisal, up to and including the interjection of violence, generally maintains a system of social adjustment and conflict management for the groups involved. However, when the system falls out of balance and is escalated out of proportion, the common interest in limiting cost and risk and returning to more acceptable levels of bargaining generates impetus toward reintegration at a higher level of social organization.

The move toward reintegrating social groups at higher levels of organization can be seen in the almost universal pattern by which murder chains arising from quarrels are ended. Whether among Albanian peasants, Bantu tribes in Africa, or organized criminal gangs, the process is virtually identical. When a killing occurs, it must be avenged by counterkilling. This in turn must be avenged, and so on as the groups involved decimate each other's ranks. In each case, the victim's gang or lineage kills a man of the murderer's gang or lineage as nearly equal in rank, age, and social standing to the original victim as possible. Otherwise, the implicit rules of mutual restraint, which still exist although a murder chain is in progress, would be broken and even more dangerous escalation would ensue. The thing is settled when go-betweens or group leaders confer and agree to restore balance.

Usually the murderer of the last victim is killed by his own group as an act of earnest; sometimes reparations are made to the families on both sides; and procedural and substantive agreements are sought to prevent recurrences. Such agreements in effect legislate bargaining rules between the groups, sometimes establishing attempts to structure relationships which now transcend the single self-help group and to transfer some of the group's sovereignty to the joint authority of both groups acting together.

Both groups now deny legitimacy to certain kinds of self-help and confrontation behavior which in the past was a usual part of their behavior systems. These remain intact between the newly integrated unit and other outside units and still remain as a residual and implicit threat which enforces the legitimacy of the new methods of bargaining. Bohannan calls this "the conventionalization of the retaliative sanctions" (Bohannan, 1967, p. 8).

Acts that escalate violence and break down mutual cost-risk constraints generate anxiety, imbalance, and a sense of incompleteness. Such acts are self-fulfilling prophecies and force other acts to follow. Children's play often rises in excitement and roughness until somebody gets hurt and cries; then it ends. The argument between husband and wife in which one impulsively raises the unmentionable issue, the sudden, out-of-context threat to run away or to inflict physical injury, threatens the constraints. All the parties to a quarrel recognize the imminence of danger when one of them violates the rules, when such such becomes such burn, such divorce, or push-kill. A desperate threat is a mark of weakness. Immediate surrender by the other side is not likely; in fact, after the sudden hush and gaping stare that follow the threat, counterescalation is the predictable response. The specter of death, the ultimate climax, enters the scene even though the substance of the threats already exchanged is still beyond his reach. Unbeckoned, the specter of death comes anyway, because the latencies of the process of counterescalation summon him inexorably. The Mexicans have a saying that "when you commit murder, you carry the dead man's soul on your back, and only your own death can remove the burden" (Mailer, 1968, p. 86), a notion which captures the sense of incompleteness, the drive toward total reintegration or toward death.

Unbalanced escalation implies that the functions and tasks of the group have changed and a higher level of hierarchical organization has become necessary in order that the groups may continue to achieve optimum values. The technology of the automobile, truck, and airplane broke down the system of local autonomy of criminal gangs engaged in bootleg whiskey production and traffic in the early years of prohibition (see Messick, 1967). Thus, the gangland wars of the 1920s for exclusive enjoyment of the revenues of big city crime were reenacted as a series of national and international gangland wars in the 1930s. Just as the earlier stage of conflict had led to new city-wide authority, so the later phase of expansion started as a series of "push me and I'll push you back" ad hoc adjustments. But out of each transaction a larger authority issue relentlessly thrust itself forward. Soon an all-out struggle for power among the well-established suzerainties of the cities was underway. Simple reprisal rules of push-push broke down. The typical pattern of escalation appeared, preceding both enhanced cost-risk warfare and eventual reorganization and reintegration at a higher level. Push-push became "push us and we'll break your backs, burn your trucks, and assassinate your leaders." In other words, escalation became an assertion of hierarchical authority based upon a presumed superior ability to withstand a test by confrontation and the use of force.

As happened in United States military stategy of the 1950s, which was based upon ideas of nuclear *first strike* and *massive retaliation*, the "push-kill" pattern of action and reaction breaks down low-grade methods of bargaining. By these doctrines, the United States sought to deter Soviet pushes and to deny the Soviet push-capability any diplomatic efficacy. However, the kill-threat promise of escalated response did not work well. The Soviets pushed anyway, and the U.S. kill-capability did not seem applicable. It inhibited push-push reaction on our part, frightening us and our allies more than it did the Russians. The result was a series of futile searches for higher level reintegration through summit talks. However, there was no redefinition of strategy based upon limited response in kind (push-push). Instead, the strategy and capability based on the assumption of U.S. dominance remained, together with a creeping and reluctant acceptance of Soviet military parity.

A declared and promised kill reaction elicits the ambivalence of all escalations. It may deter the original push, or it may cause the original pusher to kill first. In the first case, a pattern of dominance and hierarchy emerges which resolves the underlying authority question and provides the basis for reintegration, on a higher level of organization, between unequal parties. The alternative is "kill-kill," which means either unlimited warfare or reintegration among equals. In either case, an ultimate test of viability is underway; out of it must come new patterns of hierarchical organization.

All survivors of a period of high cost-risk hostilities at some point evolve and implement integrated relationships with regulatory policy-making and adjudicatory institutions. In the community of organized crime, for example, conflict of various kinds continues, but the general rules, the vantage points of bargaining, and the personnel who occupy them are changed. They are to some extent formalized, able to reinforce and perpetuate themselves. Violence is once again limited and controlled, but it still exists as a last resort for all the participants and as a means of threshold enforcement by the newly unified authority institutions. The violence functions become largely passive, maintaining common incentives which prescribe the boundaries of bargaining and dampen both the tendency toward escalation and the efficacy of threatened escalation.

The terms of this model, U.S. strategic doctrine of nuclear first strike and massive retaliation (conventional aggression or subversion anywhere in the world punishable by total nuclear destruction), are based upon an assertion of hierarchical authority, that is, U.S. economic and military (if not moral) superiority, which the Russians were asked to confirm in the world balance of power. Instead, the Russians sought economic and military parity, achieving it by the late 1950s and thus rendering the strategy both incredible and dangerous. "Push me and I'll kill you" tended to become, on both sides, "therefore, I may have to kill you first." When this point was reached, many generals on both sides called for efforts to create unchallengeable striking power and a doctrine of "preemptive" or preventive war. But saner men rejected this program. Throughout the 1960s, both nations moved toward positions of substantial military parity at reduced levels, together with a posture of *second strike flexible response*, which in effect represents a stable condition of rough political equality recognized and respected by both sides even in the face of continuing diplomatic competition and recurrent crises.

As with gangland wars, we witnessed in this U.S.-Soviet equation the breakdown of informal bargaining constraints leading to the danger of heightened violence and ultimately reintegration at a higher level. This can happen to all kinds of social groups at all levels of organization in national societies. The essential factors are the conditions that require functional reintegration: changes in the physical environment; changes in the balance of power among groups in a society; emergence of new capability for bargaining; and demands for recognition by previously silent constituencies. One might make a long list of the kinds of factors to which the ecological balance and the structures of social groups respond.

Political violence, threatened or actual, is intrinsic to the process, whether it serves to maintain low-risk patterns of bargaining or becomes a test of group and institutional viability. This is not to say that confrontation must take this or that form at this or that time. The exact tactics that are employed as threats, demonstrations, defense, and destruction depend upon the history of particular bargaining transactions, the capabilities involved, the cost-risk constraints, the intensity of interests and commitments, and the efficacy of various behavior options to bring about control, system maintenance, adjustment, or system reintegration. The exact incidence, form, and scale of political violence respond to the dynamics of bargaining. While not unrelated to the conditions of conflict (which initiate and give content to bargaining engagements), the tactical dimension may vary independently. Tactics that are found to be adaptive and efficacious tend to be reinforced, imitated, and perpetuated.

In the contemporary crisis, it must be admitted, the tactics of confrontation politics have indeed been adaptive and efficacious both in strengthening the unity, leadership, and general bargaining position of disadvantaged groups and in inducing social change. On the other hand, the preferred and less provocative tactics of political participation, petition, and peaceful demonstration, "working through the establishment," have had only abstract, legal, and token effects, have discredited leaders who advocate and use them, and have divided and frustrated the new constituencies of the urban slums.

You say you want a revolution
Well you know
We all want to change the world.

THE BEATLES, REVOLUTION 1, 1968

MEN, GROUPS, AND THE STATE

5

The state is a formal institution which seeks to acquire and legitimize a legal monopoly on violence. It is *the* macro-institution, the ultimate level of organization, integration, and authority for all social groups in a world organized in nation-states.

The process of reintegration that we have described among primitive groups, subcultures, and outlaw organizations may be likened to the process by which states that achieve legitimacy are born, demarcated, and integrated. All groups observe and enforce a security code among their members. Under conditions of confrontation and warfare, the requirements of the security code are greatly intensified; to a certain extent, every group that endures such conditions (e.g., the French underground in World War II) becomes a protostate, claiming and attempting to exercise a legitimate (although not legal) monopoly on violence. It is able to impose extreme penalties (including death) both upon its enemies and upon its own members whose actions have threatened group security.

Historically, it is not uncommon for such groups, treated as criminal conspiracies by those who claim state authority, to end up themselves (through coup d'état, revolution, separation) as cadres of a new legality and a new organization of state power. Gangs of American rabble raped and stole, rustled horses and cattle, burned Mexican villages, and became generals, governors, bankers, and large landowners in the new republic of Texas. Every group that acts as a protostate does not seek to become a revolutionary regime. Yet, in some cases, the process at work produces that result. Violence is the essential cutting edge that creates and maintains ecological separation between integrated social organizations.

This can be seen in the perennial theme of the television western. Hardened and professional gunslingers move into frontier territories. They exploit the absence of federal authority, and the God-fearing settlers organize in self-defense. Everything is touch-and-go until the federal marshal finally walks down Main Street, the U.S. Cavalry makes the scene, or a conscience-ridden member of the gang decides to go straight and is made the sheriff. In real life, professional gunslingers often became sheriffs and marshals, mayors and judges, ranchers and bankers when federal authority ultimately arrived to organize the territories. The saga of "the fastest gun in the West" in pulp fiction and television drama reflects a prestate era in which each *real* man depended on his individual prowess and bravery as the ultimate means of adjusting his relations to other similarly sovereign individuals. The "trusty six-shooter" is called the "equalizer," reflecting the bargaining equations at work in the same way that sovereign nation-states ultimately regulate their relations by trusty equalizers, their military capabilities.

Violence is the cutting edge of social integration; it is the process of demarcation and the final measurement between sovereignties. It is immanent in the process by which fetus and mother tear themselves apart into separate organisms. It is always ambivalent because it defines a boundary condition which can lead either to complete schism or to reintegration at a higher level.

The System of States

Many people argue for international law as a substitute for war as though the two were not intrinsically related. This point of view reveals a blissful ignorance of the functions of violence in domestic legal systems. A viable system based on law protects the conditions of group action. Law always rests on state violence. The threat of violence and the fear of the breakdown of law and order act to moderate demands and positions, thereby setting into peaceful motion the informal political process of negotiation, concession, compromise, and agreement (see Nieburg, 1963, p. 49). Although there is no centralized police power in the international forum, the processes of mediation and negotiation operate in much the same way. The credible threat of violence in the hands of the nations has a stabilizing effect, if statesmen attend to maintaining their national capability for demonstrating violence, and if their ambitions are commensurate with the bargaining position that their armaments achieve. More comprehensive legal codes and a world government might not improve the stability of the world community in any case, since the possibility of civil conflict exists in all political systems. Civil wars are frequently bloodier and more unforgiving than wars between sovereign nations.

In international politics, the threat of violence tends to create stability and maintain peace. Here the threat is more directly responsive to policy controls. The nation-state has greater continuity than the informal political systems that coalesce and dissolve in the course of domestic social change. The threat of violence can be asserted much more deliberately and can be demonstrated under full control, as in "good will" navy visits, army maneuvers near a sensitive border, partial mobilization, and so on. Because of the greater continuity of these macro-systems, national leaders must strive to maintain the prestige of a nation's might and will. If a nation's military reputation is allowed to tarnish, future bargaining power will be weakened. It may be forced to reestablish that prestige by invoking a test of arms that elicits greater respect for its position from other nations. All strong nations are anxious to demonstrate their military power peaceably, so that their prestige will afford them the bargaining power they deserve, without a test of arms.

Because the threat of violence is a conscious instrument of national policy, it generally lacks the random character of domestic violence. If the armaments of nations fall out of balance, if the prestige of nations is no longer commensurate with their ambitions, if the will to take the risks of limited military conflict is lacking, if domestic political considerations distort the national response to external threat, then the time becomes ripe for the outbreak of violence, which may increase until it gets out of control.

In general, the dangers of escalating international conflict induce greater, not lesser, restraint on the part of national leaders in their relations with each other. Attempts to achieve ultimate security are as self-defeating for nations as they are for domestic regimes.

The functioning of consensus and competition among nations is not fundamentally different from that of domestic politics. The most striking difference is that in domestic politics the level of centralized violence available to the state creates a high threshold of stability against the threats brought to bear within the system by private groups. In the international forum, the closest approximation to such a threshold is the decentralized forces available to the great powers. A power interested in modifying the status quo must raise the level of its threat of violence, in order to induce other powers to choose between making concessions to its demands or incurring the costs and risks of an arms race. To the extent that the established powers can and will pay the costs and take the risks, they can raise their own levels or threat of violence, thus preventing the challenger from getting any political advantages from his investment. When all the great powers are attentive to the equations of potential violence, no nation can hope to gain conclusive political advantages from an arms race. This situation makes possible international agreements for stabilizing arms and bringing about political settlements.

The distinctive mark of the state is its unitary sovereignty, which centralizes the authority of all the various normative systems of behavior that make possible the precarious balancing act of group life. This unitary sovereignty serves to protect private and public activity and bargaining through which men seek to achieve whatever values they contrive. The nation contains a vast multiplicity of personal lives, energies, relationships, and so on, which somehow must maintain order in the midst of change, and change in the midst of order; the group must endure and grow through continuous adaptation to the parameters of the human and physical environment. The power of the state gives authority to the institutions which mediate and bind diversity with unity, freedom, and experimentation, and conflict with social stability and institutional continuity. The state authority does not eliminate conflict but underpins the institutionalization of conflict and bargaining in ways which optimize consensus and values.

Political violence cannot be dealt with in terms of a "legality" which views the formal system of law and order as sacred and inviolate, a view which is easily corrupted as a status quo ideology. Legality supports the prevailing consensus against erratic transitions, enabling the majority of citizens to conduct their private and public affairs within a more or less stable environment. Private violence and forceful self-help are among the most important conditions which legal institutions are intended to replace. Yet this very value endows such methods with efficacy as the last resort of political bargaining.

The state is not a table of organization. It is the variety of private men elevated through some political process to positions of responsibility and authority in the institutions by which the regime seeks to win and hold legitimacy. A concrete and realistic model of the state is suggested by George Bernard Shaw: "The law is not executing a criminal . . . a man is killing a man" (Shaw, 1903, p. 232). The various men who win office by the complex ways of multiple conflict and accommodation always reflect diversity, divergence, interests, and loyalties representing some broad cross section of the population. The state machinery is rarely a monolithic juggernaut of unchallengeable power and discipline. The very instruments of police power are in themselves representative of and responsive to different segments of the community. Coalitions, once in power, have a way of reverting to conflicting identifications and interests

Beneath all the norms of legal and institutional behavior in national societies lies the great beast, the people's capability for outraged, uncontrolled, bitter, and bloody violence. This beast is common to both totalitarian and democratic societies. Any new group which has new bargaining capabilities, and whose interests are too flagrantly abused or ignored, is a potential source of violent unrest. This fact is a major restraint against completely arbitrary government. Even totalitarian regimes can hope for stability only if they reflect the changing currents of political interest of the people and if they are willing to recruit new elites from the potentially disaffected groups they rule. Even a totalitarian state must provide some concept of fairness and flexibility, an ability to change in response to the changing internal and external demands put upon it. In fact, to the extent that a totalitarian regime permits, or is forced to tolerate, outside political pressures, it has ceased to be totalitarian and has become, for all substantive purposes, pluralistic, regardless of its formal structure. However, the dynamics of totalitarianism make this kind of evolution difficult, if not impossible. Dictatorships of the one or the few usually raise the level of official terror in order to deter the threat of violence from below. Terror and counterterror escalate until the whole system collapses in an orgy of violence. The prospects for raising anything but another dictatorship out of the wreckage are remote.

All state systems must integrate into the power structure at least those groups who are self-conscious, organized, interested, and capable of exercising private power in some manner The notion of a totalitarian regime able to ride roughshod over practically all its citizens, enforcing dogmatic ideologies from above and preventing political change from below, is a myth. No system can long operate without legitimacy. Every regime, whatever its narrow base, its means of access to power, or its ideology, must set about building consensus somewhere—most importantly, among those who themselves retain the capability of imposing high costs and risks through concerted action if they are too arrogantly neglected.

Lasswell observes that the rule of fairness and representativeness is less important in times of international crisis than in times of peace. The severity of the task confronting the nation may enhance the legitimacy of the regime even though domestic flexibility has been suspended. However, the evidence is persuasive that even under stringent wartime rules, a regime is compelled to sustain its legitimacy by maintaining equity and representation at least for those groups and interests whose support is necessary to the war effort. Even military governments occupying hostile territory seek legitimacy in order to reduce costs and risks of occupation and to escape the hopeless route of repression and reprisals. Except when urgent military necessity supervenes, constructive pacification is always cheaper and more advantageous for the occupation authority (Lasswell, 1947, pp. 33–50).

The Role of Groups

The most striking finding of the behavioral sciences in the last twenty years is the central role in social change accorded to groups. Large or small, formal or informal (as they get larger, they tend to become more formal), they are the seedbeds and nurseries where new leaders, values, and behavior norms emerge, are tested, and are offered to the larger society. Individuals, especially the young, get left in the gaps of social change and experience a period of random behavior, which may and does lead to crime, suicide, radicalism, a testing of the established order, its options and alternatives, and its possibilities for invention. Many of them become harried fugitives in the rat maze that exists along the disorderly boundaries of conflicting value systems and groups. Sometimes enough of them gather at this or that turning to organize in groups of their own, which impose a kind of order and provide a new locus of conflict as well as another option for reintegration of the whole society.

The competitive struggle among fledgling groups for hierarchical influence is society's instrument of creative growth, of continuous adaptation and choice among various options for internal integration. The boundaries of relative disorder are in fact the key areas of conflict and bargaining among interest groups. Studies in ethology, anthropology, and political science demonstrate that competition within a dominance hierarchy need not in itself cause intense dissension and disruption. Rather, hierarchical authority, common to all group-living vertebrates, tends not only to promote general peace and order, but also to preserve the ability of the group to profit from conflict by reintegrating itself in the face of internal and external stress.

As the family is the primary biological group and the first group experience for the individual, so the social group is a secondary family.

It may be said that a college education is more important for reorganizing identifications from primary to secondary groups than it is for promoting academic learning. More learning, in the first sense, occurs in dormitories and barrooms than in classrooms.

Every person is identified with a number of social groups, each meeting some biologically conditioned or socially created need. Each of these groups is normative, in the sense that within each group there grow up standards of conduct applicable to situations created by its specific activities. As a member of a given group, a person is supposed to conform not only to the rules which it shares with other groups but also to those which are peculiarly its own.

As a member of a family group (which is in turn the agency that transmits the norms that governed the groups from which the parents came) a person possesses all its norms pertaining to conduct in routine life situations; as a member also of play groups, work groups, political groups, religious groups, he acquires norms which regulate specialized life situations and which sustain, weaken, or even contradict the norms he has earlier internalized. The more complex a society becomes, the more likely it is that a large number of normative groups will affect a person, and the greater is the chance that the norms of these groups will fail to agree, no matter how much they may overlap as a result of a common acceptance of certain norms.

For every person there is (from the point of view of a given group of which he is a member) a normal (right) and an abnormal (wrong) way of reacting, the norm depending upon the social values of the group which formulated it. Conduct norms are found wherever social groups are found, that is, everywhere. They are not created by any one normative group; they are not confined within political boundaries; they are not necessarily embodied in law.

Individuals discover, learn, and achieve values as members of groups, formal and informal, at all levels of organization of the society. Without the creation and reinforcement of normative social relations which group life affords, personal values take on a spectral sense of unreality even for the individual who holds them. Though they may originate with inspired, talented, or tormented individuals (writers, artists, managers, editors, etc.), so long as they remain the interior vision of an isolated man, they lack the test required to give them legitimacy even for their author; that is, they lack integration into some kind of group experience. What an artist achieves by flinging his work before the public, the administrator achieves by directives, memos, and reorganizations; the reformer by personal persuasion and public speaking; and so forth. In short, legitimacy is an attribute conferred by some kind of consensus. Everyone with a grievance is extremely anxious to tell his story so that he may find someone who agrees with him, thereby giving his complaint a scrap of legitimacy. The truism that man is a social animal is nowhere plainer than in his need to reinforce his self-righteousness.

Through their relationships in groups, both face-to-face and remote and theoretical, the experiences of individuals become the life history of the whole society. In values and morality, the group is larger than the sum of its parts. Every group, however small, marginal, specialized, or hostile to the values of other groups, is able to generate and sustain legitimacy. Honor, justice, and group loyalty supersede and transcend individuals. Self-preservation yields to group values when the group requires it. Every group has its heroes, legends, and martyrs, even juvenile gangs, criminal mobs, or old folks' homes.

Studies of "why men fight" conducted after World War II and the Korean war demonstrate that "patriotism" and "indoctrination" have little to do with combat performance; rather, the best fighting men were those who belonged to well-integrated small groups, squads, and companies, who valued above all things the loyalty and respect of their fellows. Spontaneous, voluntary, and informal groups are held together by the power of their legitimacy and require few negative sanctions to enforce their norms and values. Mutual reinforcement and esteem keep a futile remnant of a political party intact long after it has lost any realistic aspiration for fulfilling its original function. The admiration and respect of one's peers is a more powerful instrument for shaping and controlling the young than parents or teachers.

The group amplifies and gives meaning to the life of the individual. It shelters and protects him and not only gives him values but also makes him more effective in their achievement. It requires and, for the most part, receives loyalty, recognition of its leaders, service toward group-defined objectives. On the other hand, when it must, every group severely punishes violation of its norms, permitting penance and atonement for small infractions, and exclusion, ostracism, and even death for large ones. For all groups, the most deadly offense is heresy and disloyalty. Groups value loyalty and conformity to their norms more than any kind of talent, ability, or genius.

The smaller and more embattled a group, the greater the commitment required of its members. Of such groups Coser says, "They tend to absorb and preempt the whole personality of their numbers, whereas larger groups require only a weaker type of participation in group activities" (Coser, 1967, p. 107). The larger a group, the more pluralistic are the residual, overlapping values represented among its members. Therefore, the more specific and limited will be group demands and consensual values. A confrontation which escalates costs and risks tends to break down the unity of action groups; members are forced to make their own assessments in terms of other values which they may not share with the group. This tendency induces counterpressure against lukewarmness and may lead to external provocations to force rival groups into actions which may restore the challenger's unity.

Small groups seek to enhance their power by militancy and by wholesale mobilization of the energies and resources of their members. Some small groups become sectarian, demanding and receiving consensus and conformity in virtually all the behavior values of members; even the exclusivity and separatism of romantic attachments and marriage are treated as suspect and potentially disloyal to group values and leadership.

Tightly knit associations of professional criminals demand and get complete dedication and obedience. The Senate crime investigating committee noted that "family, religion, and country are all secondary and required to be subservient . . . ," as if this fact were immoral in itself. Obviously all groups that are embattled intensify their security codes and demand the same intensity of loyalty. The Senate report continues: "the penalty for disloyalty . . . is usually death . . . ordered for a variety of reasons . . . a grab for power, the code of vengeance, gangland rivalries, infidelity to the organization, or even for suspicion of derelictions, particularly for informing or aiding law enforcement officials" (United States Congress, Senate Committee on Government Operations, 1963, Pt. I, p. 2).

Such groups evolve elaborate and often secret rituals to dramatize the severity of their codes and to bring mutual reinforcement of unifying values to bear. From time immemorial the initiation rites of secret societies have served such functions, taking on a decidedly religious tinge. Such a rite is reported of the Mafia in Sicily. When a new recruit, after a long period of trial and observation, is admitted to membership, he is led solemnly through a candle-lit assembly of the members to a table displaying the image of a saint. He offers his right hand, and blood is drawn and sprinkled on the effigy. Before the saintly figure covered with blood, he takes an oath which binds him indissolubly to the association. Soon thereafter he is called upon to carry out an execution ordained by the association (Reid, 1952, p. 33). In the new world, according to Joe Valachi, the Cosa Nostra maintains a similar rite. The inductee takes the oath while holding a piece of burning paper, a symbol of the way he will burn if he betrays his oath. Afterward, a number is drawn to determine his "godfather," the man whom he will serve and who in turn will be his protector and his teacher (United States Congress, Senate Committee on Government Operations, 1963, Pt. I, p. 183). There is an exclusive Negro club in New York City whose initiation rite requires the killing of a white man—any white man.

Exclusion and ostracism of traitors constitute the group equivalent of death. There is a hushed anxiety and preoccupation in any group which has evoked the ultimate penalty, in the office when someone is fired, in the tavern when one of the old regulars is told not to return. Disloyalty is a challenge to the group's legitimacy and a test of the fundamental bond that holds the group together. Similarly, and for the same reason, the breakdown of bargaining relationships among groups leads to tactics of warfare primarily designed to challenge, discredit, and test the legitimacy of rival groups while reinforcing and unifying one's own. This can be accomplished by group actions of high cost-risk which cement the unity and test the commitment of its members; by expansion of the group's membership or resources or both; by the achievement of success in specific goal-directed activities. The requirements of group legitimacy help to explain many twists and turns of the tactics of protest and confrontation. In 1967, Father James Groppi launched two hundred days of open-housing marches in direct response to the challenge to his prestige and influence by teen-age groups during week-long rioting. Gangland execution may be functional in maintaining a group's legitimacy, quite apart from the choice of victim and the social significance of the action. Provocation of police brutality, arrest, and long court trials have always been methods available to radical minorities for internal as well as external purposes.

Kenneth Boulding uses the term "expansion pressure" for the condition that turns latent and passive conflict into actual conflict brought about because, in order to reinforce its legitimacy and thus to survive, the group requires growth in membership, income, territory, and so forth (Boulding, 1962, p. 154). Hazardous and provocative tactics elicit counterpressure which narrows the options of all parties, forcing those who were otherwise uncommitted to choose sides and at the same time providing access to a larger audience than the group ordinarily has.[7]

Values shared by members of a group, such as religion, race, homosexuality, LSD, nudism, differentiate it from other groups. Such differentiation itself is one of the most important functions of values and symbols. Whether such values are circumstantial or arbitrary in origin, they tend to be reinforced by each group's normative system, to be enforced by each group's authority struc-

---

[7] "Group conflict frequently exists without organization or with only loose, temporary, and informal organization. Racial conflict is often of this loosely organized character; it reflects itself in unorganized mass migrations and in individual prejudices and attitudes. Sometimes it manifests itself in temporary, loose organizations, like a rioting mob or a lynching party. Industrial conflict, likewise, exists long before its formalization by labor unions; slowdowns, ca' canny, sabotage, and strong group pressure against the worker who cooperates too enthusiastically with the boss are all marks of unorganized or very loosely organized group conflict. Indeed, almost all the phenomena that are associated with the union-management relationship can also be found among unorganized labor. Religious conflict is frequently group conflict rather than organizational conflict. Nowadays especially, churches do not openly persecute and seek to exterminate the heretic, but there is a subtle and persistent undercurrent of conflict as expressed in social discrimination, avoidance, and individual religious prejudice or preference." See Boulding, 1962, p. 107.

ture, to become a symbol of group identity and loyalty, and to become an ideology in the name of which all the tactics, strategy, and accidents of political bargaining are rationalized. Group ideologies are generalized into universal doctrines in terms of which all the problems and conflicts of the whole society may be cast and a political program formulated (Mannheim, 1936, pp. 264–309). Through the competition for formal power and influence in the hierarchy of the nation, any such doctrine may come to represent the coalition of interest groups which prevails in the bargaining process (whether peaceful or violent). The doctrine may become the ideology in terms of which the whole culture comes to interpret its hopes and fears, actions and experiences, for as long as the authority of those who represent it retains legitimacy.

The concept of group political systems, at various levels of social organization, undergoing a continuous process of conflict and accommodation lends itself to an ecological approach. The constituted government might be viewed as both participant and referee in this process—as having a responsibility to stabilize the turbulence of political change surging beneath the surface of social relationships. The two primary issues of politics—who shall apportion values (authority issues), and how they shall be apportioned (policy issues)—are inextricably involved in all questions of political relationships and can be separated only theoretically.

All human relationships, both individual and institutional, are involved in a dynamic process of consensus and competition. These are opposites only as conceptual poles of a continuum. In real relationships, it is often difficult to distinguish objectively between the two. The distinction is sharp only subjectively, for the participant, and his perception of consensus or competition may change from moment to moment, depending on his political role and objective circumstances. A political role is defined in terms of the many political systems in which the individual plays a part either objectively (by participation) or subjectively (by identification of interests). A political group operates through a hierarchy of authority and values. Each group constitutes a complex structure of leadership and influence, but because of the nature of its task (maximizing and allocating certain values), its decision-making power is usually vested in one or a few roles (the elite) at the top of a pyramid.

Formal and informal political groups exist at all levels of group life (children's play groups, families, lodges, gangs, work groups, nation-states, international alignments), interpenetrating each other among and between levels. Each isolated system has an interdependent structure of roles, involving loyalty to certain values, symbols, leaders, and patterns of behavior. The discrete individual, a member of many groups, must structure his own hierarchy of commitments to meet the simultaneous demands made upon him by many different roles.

Within the individual, the conflicting demands of these roles create tension. Similarly, within each system conflicting values among members are constantly adjusted as roles change, maintaining a state of tension. Political groups have an objective, dynamic interrelationship which is structured into the hierarchy of macrosystems. Within the latter, each subgroup has a role much like that of the individual in smaller constellations. Each may be part of several larger groupings which impose conflicting demands upon it. Consequently, a state of constant tension is maintained at all levels. This objective tension is seen subjectively in terms of either competition or consensus, depending on the comparative degrees of collaboration and conflict which exist in the tactical situation at any given moment.

Any two or more systems may appear hostile at any given time. From the viewpoint of the participants, the conceptual framework of competition overrides underlying consensus. Decisions and policies of rival elites are rationalized in terms of hostility to the values and leaders of the other group. However, if events conspire to place a higher value on a hostile tactical situation confronting the coalition of which both smaller groups are a part, their relationship will be transformed quickly to fit a conceptual framework of consensus which will override and mute the unresolved competitive elements. Such an event may also bring about internal leadership changes in both subgroups if the elites are too firmly wedded to the requirements of the now irrelevant competitive situation, or if a sign of good faith is needed.

Objectively, tension is always present among all roles and groups; that is, elements both of competition and of consensus are always present. The subjective emphasis which each pole of the continuum receives depends upon the value which the tactical situation places on acts and attitudes of hostility or of collaboration among the various systems at various times. Degrees of hostility and collaboration are structured by a hierarchy of values within and among all roles and systems all the time. All are involved in a dynamic process.

Because of the individual's role in the macrosystem of nation-states, he tends to view the Cold War in terms of competition. Similarly, because of his role in the subsystem of the family, he tends to view family problems in terms of consensus (until the system breaks down completely). One can reverse these perspectives. The Cold War can be viewed in terms of the many areas of consensus that exist between the two power blocs—for example, the wish to prevent the spread of nuclear weapons to each other's allies; the wish to avoid giving each other's allies the power of general war and peace between the main antagonists; the common interest in reducing accidental provocations; the common interest in establishing certain norms of predictability in each other's behavior. Conflict can be considered merely the means of perfecting these areas of consensus. Likewise one can view the family situation primarily in terms of competition and hostility. As in an O'Neill drama, one could dwell on all the things that divide the family members and interpret all their actions as maneuvers to subdue each other's will. Consensus then becomes a residual category, a product of conflict, and therefore of no importance. Thus one can dwell upon the collaborative aspects of international affairs or the competitive aspects of family affairs. A policy-maker should do both in the former area, just as a psychiatrist does both in the latter.

Conflict, in functional terms, may be viewed as the means of discovering consensus, of creating agreed terms of collaboration. It is impossible to reach any consensus without competition, and every consensus, no matter how stable, is only provisional, since it represents for all its members a submerging of other values. All collaborating individuals, groups, or nations make a continuous effort to exploit any favorable opportunity to improve their roles or to impose a greater part of their own value structures upon a larger political system. In an important sense, all individuals, groups, or nations desire to "rule the world" (i.e., to impose order in terms of their own values), but they are constrained by the objective limits of their own power to collaborate with others on less desirable terms and to tolerate some disorderly boundaries and residual conflicts of values and authority.

The nation-state, as a highly organized, formal political system whose structure is well-defined by law and custom and reinforced by police sanctions, develops principles, procedures, institutions, and expectations that create conditions of continuity and predictability while facilitating conflict and change. All groups within the nation-state have a political dimension and on occasion may enter the formal political process. That is why politicians are notorious joiners and seek to identify themselves with as many formal and informal groups as possible. As political entities, groups may be emerging, prevailing, or declining at different levels of social organization at different times.

Crime and violence are the preferred instruments of insurgent and inchoate political groups, value systems, behavior norms, and so forth. Some are erratic and ragged, destined to disappear; others grow in power and influence and edge into legitimacy, forming alliances with each other and with established groups (industrial, labor, political, etc.). Some have a permanent effect on society, challenging prevailing social relations and values; others exist in a netherworld of local or specialized value systems (like nudism and homosexuality) which never emerge in a generalized form to effect social change.

Syndicated crime, we have noted, is organized as a confederation rather than as a unitary system. Most gangs have only local jurisdiction and are semi-autonomous; their relationships are managed by alliances of convenience which extend throughout the country and may have international ramifications. The syndicate arose during the years of prohibition, was dominated by men of Italian, Jewish, and Irish extraction, and had strong political dimensions. Apart from the link between syndicate criminals and politicians provided by bribery, mutual interest, or coercion, the leading figures of big-city political organizations were recruited from the same ethnic groups. Before prohibition, the saloons in the nationality ghettos were organizing centers and headquarters for the growing political machines that had their bases in the immigrant population. They created a real power base which challenged existing power groups. One of the central motives of the old establishment in adopting prohibition may have been to destroy these emerging power groups in order to deny political access to the unwashed, hard-drinking, uneducated rabble of Europe who were required to work in their factories and clean their houses. As always happens when the power of the state is used to counter the rising influence of new political groups, prohibition merely drove the saloon underground, where it thrived as never before as a political factor, completing its revolution after the election of Roosevelt in 1932.

For most of humanity, the tribe or the state is the unit within which killing is murder and outside of which killing is proof of manhood and bravery. Although the modern nation-state is the technical source of sovereignty and of cohesive legitimacy, the regime that commands it at any given time may fail to establish its claim to legitimacy. Its use of the enforcement machinery of the state may merely postpone, not prevent, its demise. Cohesion purchased by force and repression only strengthens the cohesion and legitimacy of opposition groups and forces them into a statelike counterforce role.

At the nation-state level, violence is legitimate when it is used to enforce law and order, to punish transgressions against society, and to defend the state and its territory against internal or external enemies. Private citizens retain the right to use violence in defense of life, safety, family, and, in some cases, property. None of these rights is absolute; all must be exercised within reasonable limits.

Within the state, many a private group develops its own security code. Among its elements are members' reciprocal aid to each others needs, obedience and loyalty to recognized leaders, reaction of all members to an offense against one of them as though it were an offense against all, no appeal or alignment with outsiders in resolving internal conflict, and the like. To the extent that the group moves or is forced into confrontation with the state and other groups, its security code is intensified and the enforcement sanctions raised.

We have discussed the concept of subcultures of violence. Where the state is the enemy and lacks legitimacy, the inhabitants are thrown upon self-help to protect themselves and to maximize their own security. Upper-middle and upper social classes (whose interests are guarded by the authority of the state) abhor physical combat as a method of conflict resolution. They possess a wide variety of systems for conducting and resolving conflict (influence of property, force of contract, direct political influence, membership in organized power groups). They regard as trivial the social and personal stimuli which provoke combat in the milieu of the lower classes. Differential access to other forms of social bargaining and the omnipresence of state authority (embodied in policemen) contribute to the subculture of violence not only because physical violence is one of the few modes of conflict available, but also because its advantages are daily demonstrated. In the ghettos, the most serious crime is to call a cop. There is strong community sanction against this transgression because it constitutes a challenge to the prevailing and functioning systems of legitimacy. The lower-class male is socialized by a system which places the highest value on physical courage and quick resort to combat in the face of insult (Wolfgang, 1958, pp. 188–89).

In a period of revolutionary change, all kinds of otherwise moderate groups may be forced to extreme intensification of their security codes. A period of violent confrontation poses a severe test of the viability of groups. There is no substitute for the ultimate sanction of execution, assassination, and deadly combat. The irrevocable character of death gives it unique consequences. For the group, extreme actions commit a man symbolically, breaking his ties with his previous commitments and making the survival of the group synonymous with personal survival. "He is reborn, so to speak, through the act of violence and is now in a position to assume his rightful place in the revolutionary world of new men" (Coser, 1967, p. 81). Between life and death is an implicit moral judgment. In the words of a Sicilian peasant commenting on a Mafia assassination in his town, "He's dead, and if he is dead he must have been wrong. I can't help seeing it like that . . ." (Dolci, 1964, p. 45). Schelling and Hoffmann make the same point about nuclear strategy; "the act of committing oneself irreversibly," which in fact limits freedom of maneuver and might therefore be considered imprudent, under certain circumstances becomes "a source of strength" (Hoffmann, 1965, pp. 206–7).

Moreover, irreversible commitments of high risk may generate self-fulfillng prophecies, may provoke preemptive high-risk action by others, may be cheated of efficacy by being scorned by others, and so on. The threat of the ultimate sanction, death, may be deprived of any efficacy whatsoever when the intended victim either humbly accepts the risks or acts first. Thus the threat or actuality of death is not without ambiguities. Mutual threats and capabilities tend to cancel each other and create conditions of possible mutual extinction or a return to low-risk bargaining.

To the extent that the legitimacy of the state is challenged, both the regime and many private groups will assert that the use of violence is usual and proper. What tactics groups adopt depend upon which ones are available and their being reinforced by their success in changing the behavior of others. Extreme actions are by nature self-limiting, negative, and, beyond a certain point, counterproductive. They are less efficacious than peaceable bargaining through the exchange of values. Groups that lack positive values to exchange, however, will exploit what values they have. When established institutions are being uprooted and the legitimacy of centralized authority is being challenged from many sides, both the regime and other groups will be forced to violent actions. Extreme conduct will tend to become normative for all kinds of private individuals and groups. Such unstable conditions tend to advantage and bring into prominence those groups whose existing normative frameworks already legitimize the use of violence. Extremist groups seek to use violence and forms of direct confrontation in order to create situations in which such forms of behavior become normative. Success in this objective will bring these groups and their leaderships access to the bargaining process, which, under peaceful and stable conditions, they are denied.

Individuals and Anomie

To understand extreme forms of political behavior by socially isolated individuals or small conspiratorial groups, it is necessary to look at the ways in which such behavior may serve the interests of groups. Such uses may be deliberate and calculated actions of policy, initiated and directed by organized groups through their decision-making authorities; they may be the exploitation of non-planned events as a substitute or complement to such policy initiatives; they may take the form of a passive threat, an active threat, a demonstration of the threat by token action, or an effort to fulfill the threat; they may be the result of anticipated action by others or a response to such action; they may aim at provoking such action or deterring it.

Extreme tactics may be highly rational in that they tend to maximize behavior options or to preserve and augment bargaining assets.[8] Just as an attempt at suicide may be interpreted as a "cry for help," so all extreme actions may be seen as a search for or assertion of legitimacy, an expression of the will to live and love, to win human sympathy and cooperation; in short, they may be seen to arise out of the very same needs and glories of human community which maintain the normative structures of a tranquil and stable society.

The violent events of history and everyday life attract attention mainly because violence represents the frontier of our social experience, which, in order to ensure survival, must be managed and moderated by some form of control or social reintegration. The overwhelming and commonplace reality, so omnipresent it goes unobserved, is the nonviolence of the greater part of man's social life, the existence of vastly complicated cooperative activities and relationships, and the routine channeling of the great majority of conflicts at every level into peaceable and constructive bargaining outcomes.

Physical sanctions and violence may be the least important methods of social control and leadership; they are certainly the least

---

[8] In Boulding's model of conflict, rationality consists of "moving to the best position possible, i.e., the point within its possibility boundary that is higher than any other on the value ordering" (Boulding, 1962, p. 7).

effective. The most common tactic of protest, dissent, and revolution is to force upon government an escalation of physical sanctions which in itself will tend to erode the legitimacy and self-confidence of prevailing power groups. One cannot educate or mold a child or a man merely by threats of terrible punishment. Such a method may achieve temporary obedience, but the costs are high. In the long run, it will create resistance rather than compliance, and will ensure the inevitability of increasingly ineffective and self-defeating physical sanctions. At the first opportunity, the victim of such treatment will run away, rebel, or seek the remedies of spiteful self-destruction (LaPiere, 1954, p. 221).

Within a given framework of means and ends, violent behavior may be as rational and functional for individuals as it is for groups. Individual behavior can be understood only in relation to group values, interests, and norms. Even the anomic individual acts in reference to groups. Such an individual seeks reinforcement and legitimacy for his actions. "Reference group theory" has proven useful in accounting for criminal behavior. The "reference group" is "that group whose perspective constitutes the frame of reference of the actor" without necessarily being the group in which he is accepted or aspires to be accepted (Shibutani, 1955, pp. 562–63). Ralph H. Turner calls such behavior "role-playing"; the individual, even though disoriented and socially isolated, takes the role of a member and adopts the group's viewpoint as his own.[9]

Reference group behavior on the part of an individual (whether in or out of such groups) can be dismissed as post hoc alibi and rationalization. A great deal of extreme individual behavior occurs as impulsive reflex to provocative stimuli not fully comprehended by an excited actor. His attempts to legitimize his reflex will exploit any material he believes to be plausible to an auditor, and will therefore be of no diagnostic or analytic value. The dismissal of such rationalization, however, ignores a fundamental principle of *all* behavior, that is, its causes are always imperfectly understood by the actor and he always seeks legitimacy by aligning himself with such individuals and groups as may reinforce and accept him. In other words, the process of post hoc rationalization is precisely the

[9] Discussed in Schramm, Lyle, and Parker, 1961, pp. 237–38; see also Glaser, 1958, pp. 681–702.

same as the process which leads individuals to identify with groups and coordinate their own behavior with group norms. With Kenneth Boulding we may say that the fundamental principle of behavior "is much the same whether we are considering an individual acting on his own behalf or a person acting in an organizational role" (Boulding, 1962, p. 150).

One may go further and say that individual behavior always relates to group norms, even when it is directed against the values and interests of majority groups. The actor of crimes always feels himself supported by a system of values for which he is the instrument of justice and truth. He seeks recognition by his peers and goes contentedly to his doom in the electric chair, the sympathy and admiration of his peers conferring a self-image of martyrdom and immortality.

Criminal homicide does not occur in a vacuum. Study of the "choice of victim" clearly indicates that the vast majority of slayings (about eighty percent) involve people who have been socially engaged in a series of interactions prior to the crime. The series and the crime itself occur within an institutional setting (family, place of employment, recreational establishment) and generally occur among persons of similar social status. Homicides not of this type (twenty percent) fall into other recognizable social categories. A large portion of them are crimes of property in which homicide is incidental. Virtually all such crimes involve victims of higher social status than the slayers, which gives them a suggestion of legitimacy from the point of view of the perpetrators. In short, the individual exists and acts within a number of social matrices, all of which impinge on his behavior; his social situation and group identities are inseparable from his actions and motivations.

Social isolation for the individual is roughly comparable to lack of political access for the group. In both cases there is unleashed a tendency to experiment with extreme forms of behavior, as if the person or group seeks an exit from a spiritual cul de sac and a broader test of legitimacy (i.e., the ability to engage in social bargaining and the exchange of values).

The history of assassination suggests that potential assassins are frequently alienated figures not identified with organized political movements. They tend to act outside the context of prevailing cost-risk constraints which limit the tactics employed by organized groups. Lawrence Guiteau, Czolgosc, Zangara and Shrank, all of whom killed or tried to kill American presidents, were all disoriented and isolated from organized political groups. While Czolgosc and Zangara called themselves anarchists, they were not members of any of the anarchist groups common at the time. In a general revolution, their actions might have been rationalized as representing normative tactics of warfare. But such conditions did not exist at the time of their acts, which therefore must be understood in terms of a perception by the assassin that his act could create such conditions, or in terms of his subjective perception that such conditions already existed. In terms of these perceptions anomic behavior can be understood as identical to elitist behavior—except that anomic behavior occurs in a social vacuum. The stereotype of the wild-eyed anomic individual resembles that of the leader of highly embattled social groups, except for the devastating fact that the lone assassin has no followers, no organization, no group reinforcement. He is a leader acting as though he were surrounded by admiring legions. This is a kind of reference group behavior. In some cases, an extremely bold and imaginative act will in fact cause admiring legions to materialize; then the behavior can no longer be characterized as anomic—even though its form has not changed.

No one is completely isolated and disoriented, however; rather, everyone combines degrees of integration in various groups. Anomic conditions are more often characterized by conflict group identification and membership, as well as by exclusion or isolation. It cannot be said that any individual behavior is meaningless. Freud and the whole edifice of modern psychology refute and reject this view. Actions that appear to others impractical, hopeless, and unrealistic may appear quite otherwise from a different value perspective. Middle-class parents and their rebelling children regard each other in similar ways.

Children of the slums, far from being anomic, are loyal members of highly integrated groups. The delinquent is a conformist par excellence. "He is actually incapable of doing anything alone" (Miller, 1968, p. 273). He is socialized in the streets and alleys and polished in the finishing school of prison. Among thieves there is a high degree of honor, and severe punishment for lapses. That their values may be antisocial and self-destructive does not make them anomic. Quite the contrary: these values may be extremely adaptive for those who live on the disordered fringes of social systems that harass, manipulate, and exploit them, and are totally unresponsive to their needs.

Analysis of extreme behavior by individuals must proceed on the assumption that all behavior is plausible and realistic within the framework in which it occurs. To understand how a father can murder his wife and children, one begins by asking: Under what conditions would a reasonable man consider such action acceptable? Such action *might* be acceptable under conditions of seige to save them from a certain and prolonged death, or after a nuclear attack as starvation, radioactivity poisoning, and crazed and predatory neighbors close in on his backyard shelter. Transfer the analogy back to the unfortunate father: In what ways was his objective life situation comparable *for him* to such circumstances? Why did he interpret it this way? Such an approach can make extreme behavior meaningful and instructive in terms of what forms normative behavior might take in the face of extreme stress.

Each man is the hero of his own psychodrama of life. Whatever happens to him and whatever he does about it, he seeks to justify himself and his flawed nobility. He chooses ways that might justify him to others because his human nature is a socialized product. When a man is reduced to the point where he cannot salvage some scrap of legitimacy or dignity in the eyes of someone else, then, by his own hand, he carries out the informal judgment of the world, punishing or murdering himself. This resolves the puzzle of the relationship of homicide to suicide. People who are highly socialized, who have internalized the nonviolent behavior systems by which they live, tend to commit suicide; those whose socialization is weak or divided tend to react to the same stimuli by killing others. Both acts are extreme and, in some sense for the actor, are a response to an extreme situation.

Suicide may be viewed as being a reciprocal of murder and having similar meaning in terms of bargaining. Like murder, suicide is an act of killing—one in which the victim is oneself. Yet taking oneself away from others can be a means of punishing them; it can be an attempt to demonstrate a threat, and a means of influencing the behavior of others. Suicide and the threat of suicide are ancient instruments of political protest and demonstration. Hunger strikes and self-immolation are political acts with political motives and effects. Assassinations of prominent public men in situations where the assassin cannot escape are acts which beg for death, and may be looked upon primarily as acts of self-destruction in which the killing of others is merely instrumental.

Like all acts of escalated confrontation, a suicide is unfinished business for the survivors, if not for the victim. Anthropologists report that many tribal religions treat suicide as contagious for all who knew the dead man or had physical contact with the body and its surroundings. In Christian Europe, well into the nineteenth century, the church would not permit removal of a suicide's body except in the dead of night and by someone entirely unrelated to the deceased. The body was unsanctified and could not be buried near the remains of those who died an honest death by pestilence, murder, or hanging. In primitive societies it was not uncommon to sacrifice a sheep or goat to pacify the spirit of the suicide, which might otherwise draw others after him (Bohannan, 1960, pp. 110–14). In many cultures, suicide is considered unclean, and elaborate rituals are prescribed to stave off further evil. It is a common theme of literature (sometimes imitated by life) that those who feel responsible for the death are driven by remorse to take their own lives. It is not unknown in Japan for parents to commit suicide or become acolytes following the suicide of their child.

When someone commits suicide, those who sense the circumstances that drove him to it reexamine their own lives and are strengthened in convictions concerning the society in which they live. The suicide of an overextended installment buyer in Chicago led to efforts to reform state and national laws governing interest rates and the collection of unpaid installment debts. A suicide, apart from its real motives, will be quickly exploited by those with a social cause. In effect, a suicide resembles a resignation from a government: it challenges values and institutions, evoking in all survivors a sense of the unresolved tensions which surround them, threatening the prospects for their own survival. The suicide of Marilyn Monroe led within a few days to a flurry of suicides by women, most of them blond and middle-aged. Individual suicides, however obscure and ambiguous, like other acts of escalation, threaten the world and thus change it.

Extreme acts with political significance "differ from simple crimes to the extent that collective support given to outlaws is not itself the product of coercion" (Bendix, 1964, p. 45). There is some level of collective support for even the most quixotic and disgusting acts of violence. Somebody loves every assassin and rejoices at every bombing and assassination. However, the distinction between social action and simple crime or lunacy reduces itself to one regarding the extent of collective support for the action in the continuing conflicts between groups. Chalmers Johnson says, "True revolution is contingent upon this perception of societal failure" (Johnson, 1966, p. 12). José Ortega y Gasset notes the paradoxical debt to rationality paid by apparently irrational behavior: "It may be regrettable that human nature tends on occasion to this form of violence, but it is undeniable that it implies the greatest tribute to reason and justice. For this form of violence is none other than reason exasperated" (Ortega y Gasset, 1932, p. 82).

As the legitimacy of the state weakens, a host of claimants, individuals and groups, assert and offer their own substitute authority. Even in times of relative stability, there are gaps and vacuums of state authority where groups already assume semisovereign roles and exercise statelike authority. In times of upheaval and crisis the integration of the nation-state as a unifying institution undergoes major schisms. Violent confrontations involving individuals, groups, and the regime are all involved in a process of testing various claims to legitimacy. By imposing the most severe risks and costs, violence is the métier of the process, testing the resources of all the available systems of integration. This is not to say that the ability to organize and apply violence determines the outcome, or that successful use of violence is per se the basis of legitimacy. Violence is the testing instrument; it tests all the positive factors of social integration, such as the workability and success of normative systems in adapting a group to its physical and social boundaries while providing legitimate means of internal conflict. The factors being tested are often intangible and moral. Men will endure the rigors and sacrifices of violent confrontation only for what appears to be a higher good. Violence forces a mobilization of whatever assets and resources, both human and material, a social system commands. Therefore, this gives confrontation a certain validity as a test of legitimacy.

When the legitimacy of the state is weak or divided, personal leadership and loyalty become functional alternatives. The security code of groups is accentuated and converts them into protosovereign units. Where this happens, authority structures are highly personified and personalized; therefore, the challenge to that authority by other claimants also tends to be highly personal. In terms of the competition for control, succession, legitimacy, and so on, political assassination becomes a highly functional instrument, whether or not it is actually carried out. Under these conditions, threats are most likely to have efficacy in imposing restraints on certain kinds of action. Actual assassinations may be perpetrated by groups who seek to demonstrate the credibility of their threats, or by individuals inflamed by the contagions of a poisoned atmosphere.

The Search for Efficacy

To generate social change, one begins by expressing values and convincing others that the norms of behavior proposed or actually practiced are better than those already available and reinforced by society. A formal or informal group emerges which embodies the new values and concomitant behavior. Many such values get embodied in minority behavior which is frivolous and has no great impact on anyone else and no historical future. But this is the process by which values of all varieties are generated, pluralistically, somewhere in society. All these seeds of potential change become available options to the whole social system in the process of internal and external adaptation.

Conduct norms which arise in this or that group may be generalized to become normative for the whole society. This occurs through the process of bargaining which begins in the informal polity and, as the norm or the group itself attains broader legitimacy, emerges into the formal arena of nation-state politics and institutions. This is the concrete person-to-person, group-to-group dynamic of social change. There is a converse relationship between the legitimacy of state authority and that of various groups who compete as claimants for a new legitimacy. As the legitimacy of state authority weakens (through whatever cause), the pluralistic claims are proportionately strengthened. This may be considered a collective form of "search behavior." All the levels of group cohesion within the modern nation-state are available as principles of reintegration of national authority and institutions. The process of selection and consensus-building, however, is not a deliberate and linear one, but rather the result of an often tortuous bargaining process.

We have seen that each group creates and reinforces its own normative code, which reflects the interest of the group in its interaction with other groups. The most active and effective social control exists on the group level, where membership provides social and personal meaning to acts. What is abnormal conduct from the point of view of one group may be normal for another. What is normal for the whole society and embodied in law and state authority may be or may become abnormal for other groups in the society.

The legitimacy of the state is strong when its norms have high congruence with those maintained by the prevailing coalitions of active power groups, and when state authority is responsive to their changing demands, personnel, and values. When the integration and legitimacy of norms that support formal state authority are challenged or weakened (from whatever cause), other groups begin to exercise the functions and prerogatives of state authority. They tend to become states within the state, retaining an element of sovereignty which legitimizes their use of violence both to reinforce their own norms and to bargain with other groups (including the regime).

The threat to carry political dissent outside peaceable channels can distract the government from the pursuit of other values, can impose upon the government as its first and major responsibility the establishment of domestic peace and order, and can force the government into shortsighted measures to suppress violence, which may widen the base of opposition and increase the occasions for antigovernment protests.

The mere threat of private violence directed against the government therefore has very great power over government actions. By causing reallocations of the resources of the society into the essentially negative goal of internal security, the opposition is in a position to defeat or cripple the positive goals whose accomplishment might legitimize and strengthen governmental authority. To avoid this predicament, even totalitarian governments go out of their way to appease their critics. The alternative to reform is ruthless suppression, not only of the sources of the threat, but also of every symptom of united social action. Bowling clubs, assemblies of three or more people on street corners—there is no rational way to identify the first links of the chain which leads to social action. All must be broken up, and every symptom, however innocuous, must be stamped out. The hopeless search for unshakable security begins in this way and often ends with the collapse of the regime.

In democratic societies this sharp dilemma is avoided far short of infinite deterrence. The institutional distribution of authority (checks and balances, federalism, civil rights) precludes unilateral attempts to centralize all the police powers in the hands of one agent. Government can limit but not obliterate the overt threat of private violence and the existence of paramilitary forces. It must tolerate and protect all forms of peaceful, pluralistic political activities.

Violence is demonstrated, not in organized forms, but rather in sporadic outbursts. Disgruntled elites with a clear capability for causing a planned demonstration—that is, organized groups with a deep sense of moral outrage and injustice—avoid incriminating themselves and avoid provoking counteraction. They carry out "peaceful demonstrations" designed to reveal their numbers and the intensity of their commitment. These may have the bonus effect of provoking violent action against them, causing government intervention in their behalf, or causing their more inflammable followers to ignite into unplanned outbursts of violence. This potential exists implicitly in the situation.

The moderate leader is placed in a position of minimum risk and maximum effectiveness, that of playing the role of "responsible leader." He can bargain with formal authorities and with other groups of the society in this way: "You must accept out just complaints and you must deal with us; otherwise, we will not be able to control our people." While playing this role, the reformist leader may not be unhappy to have his prophecies fulfilled by a few psychotic teen-agers. Events which demonstrate violence, and thus induce other elites to make concessions, do not have to be planned. Once the emotions of a real social movement are churned up, the problem is to keep them from happening.

The irresponsible elements are, of course, disowned, but the bargaining power of the responsible leaders is enhanced. In the bargaining process, the moderate leaders often accept concessions which fall short of those demanded by some of their more extreme followers. Opportunists or "realists" often inherit the benefits wrought by the blood of martyrs. This is a healthy mode of exploiting the demonstration of violence without condoning it, enabling compromises to be reached which isolate the extremists and render them less dangerous to the body politic. Most followers in social movements will follow responsible leadership through the give-and-take of compromise because they share the general fear of unlimited violence and counterviolence, which can bring unpredictable results and defeat all rational goals. Accommodations can be reached, even if only provisionally, which preserve the forms and continuity of social institutions. Many incoherent acts of violence are exploited by insurgent elites as a means of improving their roles or imposing a greater part of their values upon a larger political system. The stronger the logical connection between the act and the ends sought, the easier it is to assimilate the act and claim it as a demonstration of the threat available to the insurgents if their demands are ignored. The rapidity with which insurgent movements create martyrs, often through the demise of hapless bystanders, and the reluctance of governments to give martyrs to the opposition are evidence of this.

The commitment required by a credible threat of violence, able to induce peaceable accommodation, is one of a very high order. Neither all individuals nor all political systems are capable of credibly using the threat of violence in order to induce greater deference by others to their values. There is general recognition by all of the kinds of values which can and cannot elicit the high degree of commitment required to make the threat credible.

Pressures for political and social change must be substantial before the threat of violence and the fear of the breakdown of law and order rise above the threshold set by the reserves of force held by the state. While threat and fear remain below the threshold, the status quo often responds to challenges to the law by more severe enforcement, more police, and enlarged prisons. But just as soon as the threat and fear near or cross the threshold, a general tendency toward nonenforcement of the law appears. The status quo interests begin to share with the disaffected groups a desire to evade and change the law, to make it conform to the movement of the informal polity toward a modified social process.

Demonstrations on the street, evocation of the risk of violence or counterviolence, disruptive direct action—all aim at creating maximum inconvenience for the social order. This is a way of influence for those who are weak in other more positive assets of social bargaining. When the basic issues at stake concern the norms that perpetuate this weakness, the road toward risk-taking demonstrations may be the only possible route of protest. The amount of risk actually taken depends upon the thrusts and counterthrusts of the situation and the patterns of efficacy.

Within the scope of approved procedures there are many tactics for dissent against the establishment. Breaking the law is not the only way to challenge or test it. However, lawful assembly and demonstration slide imperceptibly toward disruption and sit-ins. Riot conditions can be touched off by extreme reaction against dissenters, by the failures of the social order to be moved by moderate methods (which discredit moderate leadership), by the triggering of latent emotion, related or unrelated to the dissent, and, most salient, *by the implicit promise of attention and political efficacy in escalated risk-taking.* The spectrum of action available to minorities seeking confrontation is essentially a matter in which the response of the community determines the degree of desperation and risk.

Access to alternate and effective means of social bargaining is one factor in dampening much political violence. Differential access not only reflects existing hierarchies of authority and power, but also limits the bargaining options available at the lower levels. However, it is often confused with a more important factor, namely, the exigencies of the bargaining process itself—the morphology and case history of particular social bargaining transactions.

The level of confrontation and internal warfare in the United States at the present time has been enormously exaggerated. The trepidation and guilt of the established order has not prevented the use of the police power at times as an instrument of counterterrorism against the black rebellion—which deserves the most authentic kinds of reintegration of national institutions. On the other hand, the often pseudo-rebellion on the college campuses (which imitates the blacks and sometimes contains small black contingents) has been treated much too generously and has not yet been tested for real viability. Reluctance of university administrators to counterescalate has yielded the initiative to the most extreme counterescalators among the students, creating a bargaining equation that is wholly unjustified.

Today many kinds of emerging social groups are intensifying their security codes while escalating tactics of confrontation. When the real legitimacy of the state falters, the nation falls into protostate fragments and a period of escalated tactics, extremist paramilitary groups, terrorism, guerrilla warfare, and panic-prone reactions to all kind of. things. We are undergoing a period of mitosis, cell-splitting, which is also growth. Out of it at some point must come reintegration and social change. The theoretical alternative is separation and schism, ·with latent possibilities that can hardly be imagined. The high level of violence in itself creates individual and group panic reactions, inducing a high rate of political murder, beginning with the anomic acts of individuals, but passing—as conditions worsen—into professionalized ruffians and assassins serving the purposes of political groups and eventually dominating them.

The underlying and still unresolved factor of this dynamic is the black revolution. Today it provides the key to all the rest. Violence and riots may be a necessary stage of black unity before substantial reintegration of American society becomes possible. The end is not in sight.

After a month in surroundings where everything oozed filth and despair, every spoken word was a cry and every order a threat. . . .

GUARESCHI, 1951, p. 15

The cannibals really don't run the world.

MORT SAHL, WBZ, 1968

The sock-it-to-them theory of controlling frustration and anger and greed is futile and self-defeating. It isn't just unfair or unjust. It is ineffective.

DR. KARL MENNINGER, New York Times,
October 30, 1968, p. 39

POLITICS OF CONFRONTATION

6

There is no secret about the problems of our time: the oppressive discipline of world responsibility and permanent international crisis, the growing divisions between social groups, the alienation of the young, and the cleavages between city and suburb, black and white, rural slum and urban citadel of wealth and power, the decay not only of cities but also of towns and villages somehow passed by in a subsidized power economy. We know these things in the specifics of everyday life and as the problems of public policy that all institutions and groups confront daily. In politics there is no such thing as an abstract problem. Nothing becomes a problem until someone ripples the glassy surface of the social process.

A "social problem" is recognized and generalized when the available bargaining equations and established channels for adjustment fail to reflect the actual bargaining resources of the parties, forcing some groups to use pressure to get further adjustments. Problems become urgent and difficult when new constituencies, whose viability and legitimacy are still unrecognized by established power groups, become capable of exerting pressure upon the body politic. Demand for recognition and access to positive transactions through peaceable and constructive channels become the compelling goals of the new constituency. It must find its spokesmen and leaders while it develops the capability for coordinated and unified action and reaction. Those who aspire to lead must convince both those who will be led and those outside who already hold the formal and informal vantages of society. The first responses of the establishment are to deny the viability of new constituencies, to counter its emerging unity with evasion and tokenism, to use its police power vindictively, and to bend and waive its formal values adroitly in order to buy off or disarm the emerging leadership.

In short, the first requirement of new constituencies is confrontation, which inevitably introduces the danger of escalation on both sides. The viability of all the parties is under challenge, and the degree of violence is the result of the action-reaction patterns which, for whatever reasons, appear. The perils thereby evoked are an essential aspect of the learning process both for uniting the emerging constituency and for preparing established groups to admit an outsider into the magic circle of their social, economic, and political institutions.

As we have seen, the function of the police powers of the state is to maintain a threshold of force that deters or contains latent antisocial acts of individuals and groups. Some element of personal dislocation and anomie exists in the best managed and most equitable societies. Even when isolated outbreaks contain germs of larger social issues, they may be contained at acceptable costs by the measured application of appropriate police power. This is the normal function of the state in dealing with private violence. So long as this task is managed at acceptable risk and cost, police power protects most of the members of the community and enjoys general support.

This kind of violence may be termed *frictional.* To minimize and control it is the legitimate purpose of the police power. Political grievances are forced into peaceable channels and eventually adjusted through debate, legislation, public policy, and private contract.

The characteristic pattern of contemporary riots, however, has shown a tendency toward violent counterescalation against police action by elements of both Negro and white communities. While white violence has been limited, Negro violence escalates in response to police action, often with general support from the black community and with enhanced responsiveness, organization, and danger of future outbreaks. This phenomenon is different in kind from frictional violence. The capability of infinite escalation heightens the risk and increases the cost to society beyond acceptable levels; most important, it destroys the efficacy of normal methods of police power. This kind of violence must be termed *political.* It addresses itself to changing the very system of social norms that police power is designed to protect. It focuses grievances in recurring, deliberate, or spontaneous acts of violence perpetrated even at great risk and cost to the actors. The peaceable procedures of political adjustment fail to divert the escalation, whether because they are closed, discredited, halting, or simply untried.

The peculiar pattern of major social upheaval and political confrontation arises from the fact that normal police security methods become counterproductive; they merely solidify the capability and likelihood of disruption by groups which are increasingly polarized and alienated. Treating such outbreaks as frictional violence tends to create a vicious circle of violence and counterviolence which may discredit responsible leadership on both sides and make further disruption and alienation inevitable. It is these risks and costs that endow such violence with political efficacy and induce the general community to look for other remedies, not only through escalation of force but also through modification first of access to peaceable channels of adjustment and eventually of the norms of social relationships.

In the face of major political violence, the prevailing consensus of interest and power groups must choose between social-economic-political adjustments and the unpromising course of infinite escalation of force. However spontaneous, isolated, and emotional the incidents that trigger the circle of disruption, they impose an iron choice; the prevailing social order has no third course in sight.

We witness the phenomenon anew each year; it grows more perilous as imitative outbreaks proliferate, not only in the summer and by race, but throughout the seasons and as a model for disruptive action by groups of other kinds. One can readily recognize a distinctive political element which rioters seem instinctively to feel. A Dutchman who rioted against Nazi occupation during World War II noted that, like America Negro rioters, the Dutch rioters were "filled with elation by the fact that they were doing something." There was a community feeling that combined hope, impatience, and impulsiveness. They looted "to obtain trophies, not to get merchandise they could use profitably. Loot has to have symbolic value; strictly utilitarian goods are set on fire!" (Boeke, 1967, p. 577).

Scientific literature makes much of "social stress," "precipitating events," and the "contagious" quality of panic, terrorism, and other forms of extreme behavior (Abrahamsen, 1960, pp. 23–26). These are useful concepts, but they need to be fixed within social and political matrices in order to be of diagnostic value. Many studies demonstrate that social stress can be a factor of cohesion as well as of division. Under the discipline of external war, the rates of both suicide and murder fall (although suicide falls at a sharper rate than murder). The real test of social cohesion occurs under conditions of relative relief of stress. Latent divisive forces are suddenly discharged; long deferred demands for social change suddenly assert higher priorities than do discipline and unity.

Stress is not uniformly distributed in society and thus endows bargaining relationships with different degrees of commitment and urgency. If the main function of government is to "allocate values," then the inverse of that function is to "allocate stress." Groups without access to the formal process of values always get more than their share of stress; forms of direct action and political protest may be viewed as efforts to reallocate stress. Political assassination may be viewed as an act of retaliation designed to induce panic in others to match the panic already felt by the assassin; he seeks to inflict his own predicament upon others, to enlarge and legitimatize it. Langston Hughes said,

> Seems like what makes me crazy has no effect on you,
> I'm gonna keep on doing until you're crazy too.

And Dick Gregory: If the "white power structure" does not share its garbage trucks with us, "we gonna share our garbage with you!"

In the same way, urban renewal programs administered by bankers, realtors, politicians, and universities sharpen stress in the lives of slum dwellers. These programs obliterate the territory of the poor and turn it over to middle-class town houses and high-rise apartments (with token public housing carefully placed near a boundary), erasing informal ecological systems of social integration and community and liberating highly energized search behavior on the part of the displaced.

Black rioting in the 1960s has been shown by every study to be highly selective and politically acute in the choice of targets: loan companies, exploitative merchants (whose business was based upon the garnishment code), substandard tenements. "Burn, baby, burn" and attacks upon firemen have been described as "instant urban renewal"; in the sense that this method reallocates stress, the description merits consideration. The role of police terror—the "incident" which triggered the ballooning sequel—gives most of these events the character of prison uprisings. Self-consciousness and black unity were forged more effectively than in all the Selma marches. Many blacks and whites welcomed a violent test, the former to isolate and galvanize the community behind more militant leadership, the latter to eliminate the troublemakers and impose superior force in order to destroy, once and for all, the viability of the emerging movement.

This process has aided, not halted, the emerging unity of the black community. The bargaining position and demands of this new constituency are now highly viable, and therefore it must now be dealt with in other ways, including full admission for some blacks into the routine, day-by-day bargaining systems of recognized and established groups.

No precipitating event is significant unless all the factors are present, ready to react—in which case a great variety of events may be equally capable of catalytic action. Social contagion is a familiar process. When it is transitory, it is called "fadism"; and when after a long period it proves of enduring value, it becomes "tradition." There is obvious fadism in all social behavior, including suicide, crime, and political action. Men socialize each other and continuously test new forms of adaptive behavior, some of which wax and wane peripherally and shallowly, while others leave a residue of enduring institutionalized culture. The tides of social change are always influenced by creative individual acts that possess great expressiveness and communicability in terms of changing social values. Imitation and mimicry are forms of social learning having a functional effect, giving form (what might be called *behavioral direction)* to emerging values that are widely shared (Tarde, 1912, pp. 339–40). An important contributory condition to extreme behavior is the existence of social or group preconceptions of situations that require and elicit extreme responses (Lindesmith and Strauss, 1949, p. 332).

To analyze contagion and precipitating events, we must look to conditions that endow them with efficacy. To comprehend and deal with a pattern of political assassination, we must ask: How is assassination learned and reinforced? Why and for whom does such behavior become adaptive and functional? If indeed assassination should become a fad or a tradition, this would suggest conditions of deeply divided legitimacy, including incipient or actual warfare between large social groups. Once such a pattern is established, it suggests that less provocative forms of political action have lost efficacy and that, for some, only sensational political murders are still potent as rallying symbols and as attacks on the social viability of others.

Among current conditions and events that generate violence, four factors are worthy of attention:

1. The rapidity and magnitude of social change, uprooting of populations, obsolescence of institutions, of capital investment, deepening relative deprivation, and unfulfilled expectations.
2. The requirements and tasks of war and diplomacy, which generate and legitimize patterns of violence and intensify the use of formal restraints as means of social control.
3. The Vietnam war, both as a condition and as a precipitant—because of the lack of success of U.S. policies and arms, the bitter issues raised by the draft, economic inflation, and other social costs, and, most important, the loss of legitimacy by national government.
4. The black rebellion, which provides the model and the inspiration of extreme political tactics because of the efficacy of such

tactics in achieving Negro demands, in pillorying and exploiting the guilty conscience of white America, and in challenging the tokenism and evasion which characterized the response to earlier nonviolent methods.

All these factors are pertinent to the increasing incidence of political violence in America. However, uprooting by social change, war and diplomacy, and Vietnam are judged to be largely background factors capable of inducing a variety of nonviolent outcomes. Rather, *the pattern and history of black militancy is judged the active ingredient and most salient precipitant of violence.* It is this factor that has catalyzed and directed new norms of political behavior, endowing them with legitimacy, demonstrating their bargaining value to other groups, and eliciting retaliatory behavior.

The Rapidity of Social Change

Marshall McLuhan attributes current unrest and its modes of behavior to changes in technology. Violence, he says, "is an involuntary quest for identity." Every new technology sets off this quest. "Violence is directed toward image-making, not goals. . . . The Columbia students have no goals, neither do the Negroes. As long as we provide them with new technology, they must struggle for a new image" (McLuhan, *New York Times,* May 26, 1968, p. 72). He writes, "When one has been hurt by new technology, when the private person or the corporate body finds its entire identity endangered by physical or psychic change, it lashes back in a fury of self-defense" (McLuhan, 1968, p. 97).[10]

McLuhan gives us a significant and important half-truth. He emphasizes the point that is too readily neglected, namely, that technology *is* the physical environment—that human culture has created and exists within a largely culture-created set of boundary

---

[10] "When our identity is in danger, we feel certain that we have a mandate for war. The old image must be recovered at any cost. But, as in the case of 'referred pain,' the symptom against which we lash out may quite likely be caused by something about which we know nothing. These hidden factors are the invisible environments created by technological innovation" (McLuhan, 1968, p. 97).

conditions which minimize and modify the relation of social groups to the physical environment. Only occasional catastrophes of air, water, earth, and fire rupture the encapsulated, man-made world which has become the environment of human existence. Technology plays an important role in defining the tasks of culture, in providing a kind of ecological reality principle within which the options of human organization must operate.

Beyond this, McLuhan's classical simplicity is inadequate. Modern civilization and organized human groups are complex living organisms of which the technological and physical environment is as much a response as it is a condition. The direction of technology is not an abstract process, but responds to and reflects the interests and desires of those who exercise political, social, and economic power (Jacob Schmookler, 1966). The McLuhan thesis ("The Technological Imperative" cited by Galbraith) is widely shared by a coalition of aerospace industries, engineering companies, universities, government planning agencies, and so on, which look for the solution to every problem in the invention of new technology to bypass the "insoluble" human element of social problems. In the past such bypasses have served to enlarge the disparity of power between the technology coalition and the rest of us, generating many of the concrete problems we now face.

To prescribe a technological solution for technologically induced problems is to continue a self-serving process that has become increasingly sterile. The rate of "blind technological innovation" is already rapid and the ability of the technology coalition to foresee the results of cheap technological fixes is questionable. Attempts to isolate and treat the accessible physical parameters of contemporary problems will have peripheral benefits at best, serving the interests of prevailing power groups but leaving the basic social equations, the development of a new capability for social bargaining by previously submerged social groups, to fester and pullulate beneath the surface, eventually to break through and deface even the brightest and most gracious structures of our society.

It is not necessary to embrace the technology thesis in order to assess the tendency of technology to dehumanize our institutions. Hardware turnover is merely one dimension of the uprooting and turbulence of the modern age. The breakup of the family as a social group, working mothers, moonlighting fathers, the increase in all forms of crime, the vast movement and mixing of populations due to war as well as industrial development, urbanization, mental illness, permissiveness, secularism, drug addiction—all are aspects of the pathology of our times. Along with the weakening of family and informal, internalized controls comes a compensatory increase in reliance upon formal, external controls by all institutions, social, economic, and political. Large, impersonal corporations, government bureaucracies, faceless, hostile, and unfamiliar policemen strive to contain the exploding disruptions of social change; by their very method such impersonal forces generate resistance and challenges.

Jacques Ellul describes the impact of automation upon man's work, one of his primary means of self-expression and identity:

> man was made to do his daily work with his muscles; but see him now, like a fly on flypaper, seated for eight hours, motionless at a desk. Fifteen minutes of exercise cannot make up for eight hours of absence. The human being was made to breathe the good air of nature, but what he breathes is an obscure compound of acids and coal tars. He was created for a living environment, but he dwells in a lunar world of stone, cement, asphalt, glass, cast iron, and steel. The trees wilt and blanch among sterile and blind stone facades. Cats and dogs disappear little by little from the city, going the way of the horse. Only rats and men remain to populate a dead world. Man was created to have room to move about in, to gaze into far distances, to live in rooms which, even when they were tiny, opened out on fields. See him now, enclosed by the rules and architectural necessities imposed by overpopulation in a twelve-by-twelve closet opening out on an anonymous world of city streets (Ellul, 1967, p. 321).

It is not only the pace of life, and the increased insecurity that attends it, which dehumanizes, but also the monotony, meaninglessness, and anonymity of the forces that we reckon with in our daily lives. Everything is swept up by vast, impersonal, seemingly reachless, insensitive, implacable, and impregnable agents and agencies about which the individual can do nothing. To those locked in a Kafkaesque, bureaucratic prison world, the violence of a Mike Hammer or a James Bond becomes an adaptive fantasy and a model for self-defense. "Murder and capital punishment are not opposites that cancel one another but similars that breed their kind" (Shaw, 1903, p. 232). Violence is glorified in all the media of popular culture, and Gestapo types become the Good Guys. As in the turbulence of nineteenth-century European revolutions, the criminal becomes a romantic hero and the social misfit a prophet. The stock heroes of television drama and the movies have undergone a subtle change during the last generation. The nineteenth-century "rational man" (Nero Wolfe or Ellery Queen, both Sherlock Holmes types who solve crimes by the exercise of logic, aiding the duller but sympathetic police officials) has been replaced by sociopathic lone avengers who, against the wishes and interests of dumb and corrupt officials, out-plunder and out-sex everyone in sight. They beat the criminal by criminal methods in the name of abstract justice or merely for sadistic fun.

The cowboy is now rarely a simple champion of the good; he has been transformed into an opportunistic antihero, a moral loner flawed by life but justified in amorality by his bravura style, physical prowess, and basic honesty. In the words of Robert Warshow, ". . . it is not violence at all which is the point of the Western movie, but a certain image of man, a style, which expresses itself most clearly in violence" (Warshow, 1962, p. 7). When the antihero gets it in the end, we are left with the implication that not he but the world has gone wrong. The villain of the piece is often the counterpart of a hero-antihero, a "hip killer" who also has style and a code of honor based upon opportunism and physical prowess. The plot frequently contains a moment of truth: the protagonist and the villain confront each other and recognize an unspoken bond even though each must try to kill the other. Such fantasies probably vent more violence than they induce. Certainly they reflect conditions of antisocial behavior rather than causing it.

In real life, however, the children of the middle classes in great numbers have adopted the tradition of the slums that jail is not only honorable but a necessary stopping place in personal development and peer recognition. Sexual intercourse in public, nudity, illegal traffic in dope, and attacks on policemen have for some become forms of neoromantic revolutionary action. Manipulation of people "as though they are things" has been cited by Martin Luther King and others as being as much responsible for the perpetuation of grief and misery in our cities as the absence of wealth. We are baffled by the dropping out from establishment values of vast numbers of people of all social classes and ages, especially those who are beneficaries of the comforts, conveniences, and wealth generated by an expanding economy.

Mumford, always the incisive diagnostician, sees "a pathology that is directly proportionate to the overgrowth" of the metropolis, "its purposeless materialism, its congestion, and its insensate disorder, . . . a sinister state" that manifests itself in the enormous sums spent on narcotics, sedatives, stimulants, hypnotics, and tranquilizers, not alone by the hippie generation but by a great mass of middle-class adults, in an attempt to adjust to the vacuous desperation and meaningless discipline of their daily lives (Mumford, 1967, pp. 194–95).

Hiding behind palace guards of computers, punch cards, and automated production lines, giant authoritarian corporations, systems engineers, and managers create a spiritually empty drive for production and gadgetry, mobilizing all our lives to tasks that are meaningless to most of the people and thus generating alienation and estrangement. Droves of people withdraw defensively into the trance of drugs or television, or strike back wildly at the faceless social distance that destroys the possibility of creative human confrontation. The soldier activating electronically controlled missiles has no basis for empathy with his target; the industrial manager prefers to automate rather than deal with union grievance committees; state legislators delegate the problems of traffic control and waste disposal to systems engineering firms rather than deal face-to-face with the refractory human element of county boards, mayors, aldermen, and citizens.

Modern society imposes an unbearable burden on human empathy, generating personal anomie and search behavior attempts to contrive new principles of community, as well as extremes of political action. Alienation and denial of the legitimacy of the whole society become necessary defense mechanisms. New subcultures search for first-hand experience, personal integrity, and real refreshment in a world destroyed by suffocating abundance.

The dropping out of the young can be looked upon as the white equivalent of the Negro conversion from killing each other to killing policemen. The tendency of some of the most articulate dropouts to identify their situation with that of the Negro reflects both an attempt to exploit the efficacy and threat of black violence and a borrowing of the trappings, if not the reality, of black dynamism and insurgency.

The result of social alienation is increased reliance on external restraints and formal controls, methods which do not operate effectively in the absence of informal group reinforcement. Vast numbers who are poorly integrated are therefore "most likely to aggravate conflict beyond the bounds of normal disagreements" (Berelson and Steiner, 1964, p. 61).[11] In their excellent study of suicide and homicide, Henry and Short observe that "when external restraints are weak, aggression generated by frustration will be directed against the self, and when external restraints are strong, aggression generated by frustration will be directed outwardly against another person" (Henry and Short, 1954, p. 17).

The United States faces some curious paradoxes. The most productive economy in history stagnates at a high level and intensifies, rather than allays, social cleavages. The most democratic society in history witnesses political opportunities rejected in favor of violent protest. A high level of abundance and material well-being generates anger among the poor and terrible anxieties for the middle classes, especially the young. A sophisticated, advanced civilization reenacts the dilemmas of a banana republic and makes a mockery of the fondest doctrines of economic development and political stability. If for no other reason, the nation owes a considerable debt to the young radicals whose confrontation tactics are proving that MAN is not ready to become an acronym for Meaningless Archaic Nonentity! They are forcing personal confrontations on a society that has done everything possible to standardize people into interchangeable parts.

[11] "When community members are highly involved with the community per se, identifying their own future with that of the community, that identification . . . appears to modify and constrain the disagreement. People who feel apart, and unidentified, are quickest to overstep the bounds of legitimate methods and carry the dispute into disruptitve channels. When there are few or none who are identified, then there are essentially no norms to restrain the opposing sides. Conversely, if most people and organizations in the community are identified with community as a whole, then the potentially disruptive effects of the dispute are felt by all: there are conscious attempts at reconciliation" (Coleman, 1957, p. 21).

War and Diplomacy

These characteristics of culture in the United States constitute a cluster of variables having two major impacts upon the norms of political behavior. First, they intensify the rapidity of social change and the uprooting of established institutions. War, hot or cold, and permanent international crisis thrust upon the nation unavoidable tasks and priorities of defense preparedness and international responsibility. In an atmosphere of tension and crisis, all elements of spatial and social mobility are accelerated, solid social structures are dismantled and new ones jerry-built. Populations and life situations are scattered by the winds of events. Insistent demands of national security disrupt the order of personal life and rest the whole social balance upon the shifting knife-edge of each new foreign crisis.

Second, war and diplomacy provide a pattern of national behavior which by its very nature legitimizes violence in all its forms. This necessarily must inflame private behavior, raise the level of social irritability, and weaken inhibitions against personal violence. In addition to the two great wars of this century, the world since 1945 has seen 12 limited wars, 48 coups d'état, 74 rebellions for independence, 162 social revolutions, and vast numbers of racial, religious, and nationality riots (see Sanger, 1967). Respectable men in the nation's highest offices play the game of "Chicken" with brinkmanship nuclear diplomacy, and the same sport tends to become commonplace in all kinds of domestic political situations. Guns become status symbols and elemental protection for homeowners and shopkeepers, just as missiles do for nations. Ministers, teachers, and leaders urge the people to peaceable conduct and love while at the same time they support mutilation and murder abroad. Confrontation diplomacy pursued in the national interest cannot help but proliferate confrontation politics among interest groups at home. Gestapos, GPUs, CIAs, espionage, subversion, and all forms of official undergrounds facilitate and legitimize a social and political underground at home.

Such facts of life, indisputable and honored, make it easy for many people, especially those whose interest it serves and those who are young, to accept uncritically the scenario of an international assassination chain carried out under official auspices. The script reads from Lumumba to Diem, Diem to John F. Kennedy, John F. Kennedy to Malcolm X (who commented about Kennedy's death that "the pigeons have come home to roost"), Malcolm X to George Lincoln Rockwell, to Martin Luther King, to Robert F. Kennedy . . . and the next act in the series is already in preparation. Thus the series is legitimized. Thus it becomes reasonable and necessary that the next great political sensation involve another major assassination. Thus the pattern is generalized and escalated as other groups and individuals, aspirants to political attention and efficacy, deliberate which victim deserves and will best serve their purpose to get into the act.

Hannah Arendt calls our time "a period . . . of bloody imperialist adventures" which give rise to a moral dissent which is "treated with open contempt by the administration." Taught in the school of the civil-rights movement, the opposition "took to the streets, more and more embittered against the system as such" (Arendt, 1968, p. 24). Western self-righteousness in two world wars imposed formulas of unconditional surrender and total victory, in the name of which whole societies were smashed in Europe by bitter-end warfare, and in Japan by saturation fire-bombing climaxed by Hiroshima and Nagasaki. Long ago George F. Kennan argued the difficulty with which mass societies, especially democratic ones, conduct international diplomacy and wage war. Unless the nation is whipped into an ideological crusade, limited war and limited diplomacy (measured against political objectives) are virtually impossible to sustain. If this dismal assessment is correct, it might be said that an essential link exists between domestic violence and violence unleashed abroad: the latter must overreact in order to be justified to American public opinion; this in turn facilitates overreaction on the part of those who oppose what they consider the unwarranted use of force.

The Lingering Unsuccess of Vietnam

Vietnam is frequently cited as the most immediate precipitating event in the whole pattern of violence sustained and legitimized by contemporary war and diplomacy. Much of the so-called moral issue which surrounds opposition to the war is attributable to the failure of policy to achieve minimal U.S. objectives at acceptable risk and cost within a tolerable time, rather than to the substance of U.S. policy in Southeast Asia. Be that as it may, the term "credibility gap" is essentially a way of describing the loss of legitimacy of the national government and the incumbent administration. All kinds of unresolved issues, some related, others remote to Vietnam, share in the collapse. The critics and opponents generalize their assault, exploiting the disaster of official policy as a means to attack and weaken the "establishment." Every disaffected group sings the unsuccess of Vietnam in order to advance and argue its own values and to assert its own new principles of reintegration and legitimacy.

Certainly major failures of national policy have the effect of weakening the legitimacy of institutions and leaders. The direction of the revolt, however, reflects all kinds of conflicts that preceded Vietnam and that do not require a major foreign policy failure for validation. The Vietnam issue may really be just a target of opportunity. This is not to minimize the fact that the war has intensified all the elements of an uprooted society. The requirements of military service, the tremendous mobilization of national resources and money, the wave of inflation, with consequent dislocation of lives and savings for vast numbers of middle-class Americans, and the postponement of positive public programs to deal with competing priorities—all have embellished existing tensions and tendencies with a galloping fire. In this sense, Vietnam may be considered both a precipitating event and a background condition.

The role of the precipitant of violence may vary enormously in significance; we can assess its causal importance only in terms of the whole dynamic system of which it is a part. To quote MacIver, "The causal efficacy we impute to any factor will always be contingent not only on the other factors, but also on the dynamic interdependence of them all within the total situation. It is only as a temporary heuristic expedient that we can select any item as 'Cause' and speak of the rest as 'conditions'" (MacIver, 1964, p. 425).

None of the factors or conditions noted above, taken separately or together, are sufficient to cause extreme political behavior and violence. The increasing incidence and incipient normalization of violence by many different groups require something more—a demonstration of its efficacy as a form of social bargaining.

The Black Rebellion

It is in the black rebellion that such tactics have emerged as most efficacious. Here they have achieved a degree of legitimacy which invites imitation by every excluded social group, ranging from the Students for a Democratic Society to American Indians, Puerto Rican high-school students, and teachers. A specific coincidence of historical circumstances has made the time ripe for Negro self-consciousness and concerted social action and has also predisposed other claimants for political access to emulate Negro success.

No hypothesis of "organized conspiracy" and "outside agitators" is required to explain the clear pattern of escalated violence and counterviolence that has accompanied the search for identity, organization, and leadership by the black community. Nor is the theory of relative or absolute deprivation a satisfactory explanation. Rather, the direction of the black power movement has been largely a result of the response by dominant white power groups to early low-risk tactics of nonviolence. The process by which radical militants achieved legitimacy and entered the mainstream of Negro leadership has been largely dependent on the tokenism, evasion, and resistance which discredited the legalistic approach of the NAACP and the nonviolent methods of Martin Luther King. To the shame of the white community and its leadership, riots and insurrectionary sniping are accomplishing breakthroughs that seemed impossible before the long hot summers of the early 1960s. Even backlash and the rise of white extremism confirm and augment the efficacy of black militancy, endowing it with a defensive justification and raising the level of cost and risk for the whole society, thereby forcing the middle to seek real social adjustments as the only means of isolating, limiting, and containing the dangers of continued escalation.

Like the decades of violence that accompanied the organizing phase of the labor movement, the initial series of confrontations between the black community and the police represented an organizing phase whose primary function was to unite the Negro community and discredit both white liberals and Uncle Toms who had previously claimed to act on its behalf. "Black is beautiful," black power, and black separatism are tactics of unification rather than program goals.

In their initial response to militancy, white policemen sought to punish the whole community, treating all Negroes, including bystanders, as rioters and looters—as if, by terrorism, to teach the whole black community the futility of violence. This was a test of legitimacy which the white policemen lost; instead, their actions aided and abetted the organizing process. Training programs were put into effect to teach police and the National Guard to deal with rioters selectively, in an effort to isolate lawbreakers. Aggressive and terroristically inclined policemen were removed from ghetto assignments, and other efforts were made to legitimize antiriot measures—for example, new forms of token participation in policy-making, poverty programs, and police review boards.

To a certain extent these measures succeeded. They forced militants into more extreme tactics which divided the Negro community. However, these actions were not all of one piece, and, by and large, the conditions of social exclusion and isolation remained in force for most Negroes. Once again, the power structure played into the hands of the most militant. The division of the black community aided the process of tightening militant control, splitting off mostly those already discredited by the failure of legalistic and political tactics. As was noted by the Kerner commission, the gap between black and white is widening despite Negro gains.

Most of the adjustments have been token or abortive. Every institution in the nation is anxious to train, hire, and upgrade Negroes in white collar, professional, and junior executive jobs, but these jobs are not numerous, and blue-collar and unskilled employment is unstable and shrinking. At the lower levels, most of the work produced by crash programs involves "dead-end" jobs which only serve to confirm black alienation. Jobs on the higher social scales still tend to be for purposes of display in the front office and in full-page ads in slick magazines. Manipulation from the top down —paternalism—is still the rule. General Motors and Xerox are using a few black faces as a way of writing "soul brother" on the door in hopes that marauding bands of the still excluded group will pass them by. Negroes still account for most of the executions carried out for capital crimes, while white criminals wait on death row for long years until a court or governor finally commutes their sentences. Negroes may escape from the old ghetto compound, but the city itself becomes an enlarged ghetto encircled by white suburbs burbs with token integration, civil defense armies, all-white police forces, and armed housewives. The tax base of the cities erodes as industry follows its executives and blue-collar workers out of the city; mercantile business disperses and clusters in shopping centers. Years ago, cities ruled by white majorities fought for adequate apportionment and representation in state legislative bodies, jealously resisting programs for metropolitan and county-wide government; now, as the suburbs become the locus of power, reapportionment of state legislatures is achieved for suburbs at the expense of cities. Programs for metropolitan government suddenly seem politically feasible as a means to circumvent black political control of cities.

The disparity between city and suburb goes far beyond race and income. Every available indicator of economic activity dramatizes the deteriorating competitive position of the city—medical care, hospital facilities, private and governmental services of all kind, unemployment (which is double that of suburbs), disease and death rates, decline of housing, streets, and the rate of gas-line leaks and explosions.

A major reason why more enlightened police tactics have so far failed to end extremist black provocation is that tactics of limited force are difficult to implement and ineffective against sniping and guerrilla tactics. There are extremists in every community. By reacting against a whole community in order to deal with isolated acts of provocation (as has historically been done), the power structure endowed extremists, both white and black, with a power over events they could attain in no other way. Even today almost any irresponsible teenager holds in his hands the power to start an incident at any time. Escalation and counterescalation are built into the situation, and the Negro community is forced to support the acts of its own extremists. For decades police have responded to the acts of Negroes (including children) as though a state of undeclared war existed between the two communities. They interpreted their duty as requiring them to intimidate and terrorize at every opportunity, creating an automatic riot syndrome which could be triggered by any claimant to leadership, irresponsible youth or irresponsible policemen. It was and still is impossible for policemen to arrest one black man without having to deal with all the bystanders as though they were equally guilty. One cannot undo in a year or even a decade the automatic syndrome which a century of police terrorism put into the hands of the newly awakened militant leaders.

Lynching and the murder of civil-rights workers lost their efficacy in the South in the early stages of the civil-rights struggle. If three civil-rights workers are murdered today, ten more appear tomorrow. If one uppity nigger is lynched, ten more aggressively taunt their white masters the next day. In the 1960s, police terrorism has equally lost its efficacy in the cities of the North; however, black militancy continues to enjoy the new-found efficacy of extreme tactics, programs, and paramilitary brigades—both to maintain unity of new organizations behind new leaders and to facilitate bargaining with dominant social groups.

The year 1968 has been saluted as the year in which no major riot occurred. The great cities that had exploded during the previous five years were quiet except for isolated sniping attacks and hit-and-run guerrilla actions against police and property. Only a number of middle-sized hinterland cities, previously untouched, experienced the familiar pattern of burning, looting, and attacks on white motorists and police.

Many explanations have been offered for the relative calm. The black community has now achieved self-consciousness and a capability for acting in concert and new forms of activism are underway. "Operation Breadbasket," growing out of the Chicago program of the Southern Christian Leadership Conference, and similar organizations in the style of Saul Alinsky, are creating new institutions to administer private and public ventures and initiating every kind of pressure activity which will yield concrete and specific results: use of rent strikes by tenants' unions to enforce sanitary and fire codes against absentee landlords; pooling of savings to establish

sity presidents, city councilors, television MCs, they begin by calling their hosts "pigs" who will be destroyed when the time is right. At universities throughout the country, black student unions demand not only courses in Afro-American history and culture, but also relief from grades and abject apologies and confessions by college administrators for white racism. How can a university president refuse to negotiate just because he is called "pig," when he believes the alternative is escalated violence and counterviolence with no clear resolution in sight except massive outside police presence, which may destroy the university quite as completely as could ransacking students.

The Columbia-Berkeley model and the ghetto riots terrify authority and encourage a brutal travesty of legitimate demands for reform. Ghetto rumblings and white guilt, much of which is warranted, create a condition as unreal and unproductive as the old system of tokenism. It may be that new tests of unity, determination, and purpose are in the offing as the very success of the black rebellion stiffens backs in both communities.

The second effect of the new bargaining capability is, while ambivalent, more hopeful. Tokenism carried far enough becomes real integration, on the job, in government and politics, if not in neighborhoods or country clubs. All the new institutions arising under black initiative and leadership will inevitably become formalized vantage points for social, economic, and political bargaining, not in abstractions and slogans but in the nitty-gritty that constitutes assimilation. Programs for integration have now apparently been deferred while a stage of voluntary separate development and self-rule enables the American Negro to establish a collective identity of his own. Eventually it may no longer be necessary to insist on black pride and "Black is beautiful." Americans, both black and white, will live it by treating each other as individuals and human beings rather than as symbols of hostile communities. Social integration may come quietly and solidly on the basis of individual freedom and opportunity rather than through programs based on color. For the present, there is widespread incentive in the black community to continue to marshal its forces, removing the remnants of formal exclusion and inferiority while bargaining for other forms of access. These contrary trends, taken together, are substantial grounds for optimism. Most studies of the black community indicate that in the mass the Negro is far less revolutionary in his outlook than some of his more militant spokesmen. "While there is no doubt that Negroes want change and some of them are prepared to do desperate things to bring it about, the changes they have in mind are essentially conservative in nature. The great majority do not propose to withdraw from America; they want equal status in it" (Campbell and Schuman, 1968, p. 61). Furthermore, much initiative still lies in the hands of dominant power groups who, quite apart from racist sentiments, cannot ignore the real bargaining power achieved by the black community. A united black community is bound to have a good effect in inducing the kinds of change which ultimately will make "blackness" relevant neither for the nationalists nor for the bigots.

Mimicry and Instant Revolutions

Two tendencies are now at work for other groups as well: an effort to exploit potential black violence for their own purposes, and imitation of the pattern of protest as the means of unifying other claimant groups and winning attention for their demands.

Just as every energetic pressure group capitalized for years on the Cold War, the Soviet sputnik triumph, the space gap, the Chinese peril, the international Communist conspiracy, just as educators, scientists, industrialists, and military men all offered special-interest formulas to save the nation, so the explosions in the ghetto have provided new self-serving slogans for all groups. A massive black army of potential seditionists, saboteurs, and Mau Mau terrorists is evoked for a wide variety of ends.

Prevailing power groups exploit the urban tragedy to maintain their own advantages, reiterating that the path to progress is via more money invested in scientific and technical innovation, new government contracts to renew the slums, operate job camps, train and rehabilitate black workers, and maintain an expanding economy based on government subsidies and tax advantages, all of which will bring about a painless solution without curtailing existing property rights, righting social inequities, or modifying the disparities of political power.

So too, teachers and public employees escalate the use of strikes and demonstrations. The welfare poor and college youth exploit the methods and summon the image of the black rebellion, suggesting that denial of their claims will lead to the same escalation that only the numbers and solidarity of the black community so far make credible. A violent confrontation between Vietnam protestors and police raises the specter of an even more dangerous uprising in the black ghetto, now no longer disorganized and self-destructive, but galvanized under paramilitary organizations.

In this setting, violent confrontation becomes more frequent. All kinds of groups seek organization and legitimacy by probing and testing the established authorities and searching for opportune issues around which to rally and extend their leadership. The escalation of sensation will, they hope, win political efficacy by evoking the dangers of reciprocal extremism. It is said that all things happen at least twice. Dissenting groups all around the world have learned the words and are singing "We Shall Overcome." Huk insurgent groups, calling themselves "Beatles," grow in size and make daring attacks against Philippine troops in Central Luzon, while their balladeers sing Muddy Waters and Chuck Berry songs. Sometimes imitation converts the brilliant and the tragic into the farcical and the stupid: witness recent destructive rampages by elementary school children in Boston, Chicago, and New York City.

In much the same way, young, white, middle-class rebels adopt the successful tactics of the blacks, searching for rallying cries and issues (student power, sexual freedom in the dorms, drugs, Vietnam) with which to unify a constituency and win legitimacy. In effect, they seek once again to exploit the sacrifices of the black community for their own purposes. Rennie Davis, Yippie activist, articulated the method in the *Village Voice:* "The goal? A massive white revolutionary youth movement which, working in parallel cooperation with the rebellions in the black communities, could seriously disrupt this country, and thus be an internal catalyst for a breakdown of the American ability and will to fight guerrillas overseas" (Davis, *Village Voice*, October 10, 1967, p. 2).

Traditional "rites of spring" of the young become stylized beer riots in LaCrosse, Wisconsin, beach riots at Fort Lauderdale, occupation of university buildings, disruption of classes, and more. Assassination and counterassassination of college student leaders, as well as of government officials, has long been a feature in many Latin American countries. It can happen here! We already have witnessed bombings and burnings on several campuses. Just as strikes and purposeful property damage are filtering down through the high schools and grade schools, so extreme forms of escalated violence can spread throughout the society if we are imprudent enough to let it happen. The power to direct and control these events lies more in the hands of the powerful than it does in the rallying cries and ambitions of the powerless.

The black rebellion has created an atmosphere of anxiety and incipient terror which is making possible important, but not necessarily positive, social adjustments. This national mood creates opportunities for all those with a grievance to take advantage of the beseiged and embattled condition of traditional power groups. There are many just causes and real problems which give rise to dissent. However, there is also much that is shallow and transitory. After a well-publicized kidnaping, all kinds of people send their own ransom notes trying to cash in. Similarly, in a period of general anxiety, all kinds of people use innuendo and direct threats to exploit the opportunities created by the acts of others. Anonymous telephone and letter threats of assassination proliferate, but they have little social effect.

The best way to dampen pseudo-terrorism is to deal effectively with the roots of real terrorism; the best way to limit the mimic search for instant revolution is to deal effectively with the sources of real dissent. This may require a showdown to test the legitimacy of demands, and thus may deny automatic efficacy to extreme tactics. Courage and cool assessment of one's own resources are indispensable to formal authorities. However, superior force alone plays into extremist hands; to deny efficacy to violent tactics and leadership requires genuine validation of other channels of protest, two-way communication, and social change.

While many have learned the lesson of black power—intransigeance and stylized violence—not all the imitations are meaningless and marginal. Much of the search behavior of contemporary youth can have great reintegrative power for the whole society. Has monogamy failed? Have universities failed? Is there a need to improvise new bases of community to replace the fragmented anomie that exists in the rootless suburbs? Are job and work still adequate bases of human identity in an age of automated abundance? Is it perhaps true that the Protestant ethic *is* ready for the dustbin, and that some new ethic based upon consumption, self-indulgence, and sensuality is ripening? Is the time ripe for dismantling the great concentrations of power imposed by sheer machine production and the nation-state system? These are real questions; they deserve to be approached with open minds and a willingness to permit experimentation and social invention by those who would change the accepted order.

Irving Kristol declares that the hippies and associated sects are the only truly radical groups in American society today because "they are dropouts from the revolution of rising expectations and reject the materialistic ethos that is the basis of the modern social order." However, he despairs that simple hedonism can make a radical alternative viable. The self-proclaimed radicals are mainly concerned, like the rest of us, with consumption, "even if they prefer sex and drugs" rather than detergents and automobiles (Kristol, 1968, pp. 174–75).

Revolution is a serious business. Apart from the black rebellion, how serious and cataclysmic is this "era of confrontation politics"? How well will SDS stand up to the backlash of an S.I. Hayakawa? There is an ersatz quality in the new middle-class underground. The safety valves of American pluralism are still functioning and rob it of much of its steam. If the new underground were truly revolutionary, would we see Head Shops selling trinkets in every respectable suburb? Would Country Joe and the Fish or the Fugs be building up investment portfolios? Would Tom Hayden and Abbie Hoffman be making the rounds of the radio and television talk shows? Would underground newspapers (full of Zen Buddhism and four-letter words) have a national news service?

Death and Transfiguration

Attempts to obliterate all occasions and possibilities of political and personal violence are unrealistic and even dangerous. Any effort by the state to obtain an absolute monopoly over violence leads inexorably to totalitarian repression of all activities and associations which may, however remotely, create a basis of antistate or anti-establishment action. The logic of such attempts generates a strong counterreaction. In addition to forcing opposition into the most extreme channels (the very thing the state seeks to eliminate), a repressive system threatens the freedom and safety of every citizen. A democratic system must preserve the right of organized action by private groups and accept the risks of an implicit capability for violence. By permitting a pluralistic base, the democratic state enables potential violence to have a social effect and to bring social accommodation with only token and ritual demonstrations, facilitating a process of peaceful political and social change.

The good society must learn to manage constructively some degree of violence and potential violence. Communities can endure even with societies practicing organized murder in their midst, providing the institutions of the whole maintain their legitimacy and are able to isolate and control the effects of antisocial actions. One can never hope to eliminate completely anonymous telephone or letter threats to authors, public personalities, and people who got their names in the paper. Political assassination cannot be eliminated once and for all by any preventive measures which are not even more dangerous to the health and survival of the nation. Attempts to make violent confrontations impossible are incompatible with a free political process and may in fact enhance the probability of a coup d'état. The most anxious man in a totalitarian system is the dictator, just as the most anxious man in a prison is the warden.

However, it is possible for society to manage its problems in such a way that no single man can change history with a single bullet. The inefficacy of political extremism is the best safeguard against the danger that an isolated act will begin a self-perpetuating series and provide a pattern for political success.

At all times, even in a healthy society, the whole spectrum of political options is occupied by groups and individuals who claim leadership and legitimacy. The best way to keep the extremes of the spectrum from overwhelming the center is to improve the efficacy and legitimacy of such modes of political action and leadership as will deescalate latent threats of violence and facilitate social change and political integration of new groups. The very success of peaceable modes of bargaining constitutes a prediction of futility for extremist modes. When violence occurs, the vast multitudes of the nation will support the actions of the state in limited and reasonable deterrence, localization, and, when necessary, containment by appropriate and measured, but not overreactive, means of force. George Wallace's threat to run his car over demonstrators tends to escalate and legitimize political violence. Mayor Daley's instruction to police to "shoot to maim" looters has the same effect. Government must learn the value of nonviolence as an appropriate tactic of control in certain conditions where violence, even the superior violence of the state, will not work.

It is a simple matter to make a theoretical diagnosis of the conditions and causes of political violence. It is much more difficult to know, as a matter of practical policy, how to avoid social trials by ordeal. How does government terminate and stabilize a period of search behavior and confrontation? How to conserve and integrate adaptive social innovations? How a social process starts and spreads has been much more studied than how it terminates. A process may cease because it has exhausted itself. Some processes may go on indefinitely, ceasing only with the disappearance of the groups whose interests they served or opposed. In some cases, a process provides built-in opportunities at which it can be deliberately stopped or redirected. What should be done in a situation where high-risk political confrontation is already well established and seemingly irreversible (a situation which the nation has not yet reached)?

One can create countertendencies to dampen extreme oscillations. This calls for highly creative political action and leadership, not only from leaders of prevailing cadres and groups, but on every level of social and political organization in both the formal and the informal polity. This kind of action may not be as difficult as it appears. There is a strong tendency in social life toward humanizing power, toward creating conditions of predictability and order in the midst of change, and avoiding the danger created for all by efforts to apply overextreme penalties and measures to some. One of the great facts of American response to the recent series of political assassinations has been the tendency of the community to unite against all varieties of extremism, to seek new routes of conciliation and social reform. This is a built-in corrective which, with a little luck, can see us through grave situations.

The rise of revolutionary conditions testifies to the absence or disuse of other channels of political change. Political leaders must keep such alternatives alive and responsive to claims by newly articulate groups. Organized conflict groups tend to use less violent means of combat and bargaining than those which lack organization; therefore, we must seek institutions which offer representation and identity to groups that might otherwise remain inchoate and therefore unstable.

The nation-state is a complex living organism whose growth tends to respond to the interests and desires of those who exercise political, social, and economic power. Most of the great political problems that confront us arise when a previously submerged group acquires new capability for social bargaining. Institutions that serve only established and prevailing power groups will always leave basic social equations to fester beneath the surface of established power. Our institutions must aim at the discovery of new constituencies and new routes of access by which they can generate their own leadership. This is a very real challenge to our ingenuity as political innovators.

In terms of political power, there are no abstract issues, only "who gets what, when, and how?" and "who's doing what to whom?" All situations, however desperate they may be to some, are manageable and tolerable for those who do not suffer them. So long as slum occupants confined their crimes to the ghettos, internalized the disarray of their lives through mental disease or use of narcotics, there was no problem for most of the society. However, with the arrival of self-consciousness, militancy, and incipient organization, the heat is on. Metropolitan pathology ceases to be an abstract issue to be safely exploited, studied, and pacified; it has become the most authentic confrontation of our day. The same might also be said of other new groups that are winning self-identity and organization. When this happens, cheap fixes and evasions no long serve. Even counterinsurgency and police repression become provocative, ineffective, and self-defeating. Procrastination, tokenism, all the tricks in the old political bag are bankrupt and outworn culturally, morally, economically, and politically. Those who are already articulate and enjoy some assets of social bargaining have a responsibility to save themselves by saving all.

On the other hand, it is futile to sentimentalize either problems or remedies. Conflict, like the search for order and stability, is inevitable in social life. When the priorities of one conflict are somehow terminated, we can be certain that others will take their place, and that they will be as dangerous and insoluble as the ones they replace. To live is to grow, to grow is to strive, to strive is to struggle. We must be sophisticated enough to understand the imperfect justice of all human relations, past, present, and future. It is the unfinished nature of our task that generates the dynamics of politics and gives individual freedom its meaning. Justice is not to be had for any except as the rigors of political bargaining give it status and degree for those who prevail in the shifting compromises of the bargaining process.

Problems of race, like other problems, may be insoluble in the short run. The best we can hope for is to create a sense of movement and a faith in the ultimate efficacy of political solutions. A sense of movement toward solutions is the great thing that generates excitement and nourishes hope. It is the ultimate means of preserving the legitimacy of a whole society.

There has never been a time which was not intensely difficult and perplexing for most of the people of the world. Today's problems always appear immense, while those that appeared the same way a year before are largely forgotten. Is the prevalence of confrontation politics a sign and a mark of schism in the soul of America? The impending end? The answer to this naive and alarmist question is a paradox: conflict is always present in human relations and constitutes a great force in keeping things loose, capable of adaptation and adjustment, ready to endure other trouble-making generations. Political confrontation is "what societies do instead of committing suicide" (Kopkind, 1968, p. 54). Death and transfiguration are the countermotifs of life and growth.

REFERENCES

ABRAHAMSEN, DAVID. *The Psychology of Crime.* New York: John Wiley & Sons, Inc. 1960.

ARDREY, ROBERT. *African Genesis.* New York: Dell Publishing Co., Inc., 1967.

―――. *The Territorial Imperative.* New York: Atheneum Publishers, 1966.

ARENDT, HANNAH. *Between Past and Future.* New York: The Viking Press, Inc., 1961.

―――. "Lawlessness Is Inherent in the Uprooted," *New York Times Magazine,* April 28, 1968.

AUDEN, W.H. "Law Like Love," in *The Collected Poetry of W.H. Auden.* New York: Random House, Inc., 1945.

BEDAU, HUGO ADAM, ed. *The Death Penalty in America: An Anthology.* New York: Doubleday & Company, Inc., 1967.

BENDIX, REINHARD. *Max Weber: An Intellectual Portrait.* New York: Free Press, 1962.

BENSING, ROBERT C., and OLIVER SCHROEDER. *Homicide in an Urban Community.* Springfield, Ill.: C.C. Thomas, 1960.

BERELSON, BERNARD, and GARY A. STEINER. *Human Behavior: An Inventory of Scientific Findings.* New York: Harcourt, Brace & World, Inc., 1964.

BIENEN, HENRY. *Violence and Social Change.* Chicago: University of Chicago Press, 1968.

BLAU, PETER. *Exchange and Power in Social Life.* New York: John Wiley & Sons, Inc., 1966.

BOEKE, JAN. Letter to the Editor, *Science,* November 3, 1967.

BOHANNAN, PAUL, ed. *African Homicide and Suicide.* Princeton, N.J.: Princeton University Press, 1960

―――, ed. *Law and Warfare: Studies in the Anthropology of Conflict.* Garden City, N.Y.: The Natural History Press, 1967.

BOULDING, KENNETH E. *Conflict and Defense: A General Theory.* New York: Harper & Row, Publishers, 1962.

CAMPBELL, ANGUS, and HOWARD SCHUMAN. "Racial Attitudes in

Fifteen American Cities," *Supplemental Studies for the National Advisory Commission on Civil Disorders.* Washington, D.C.: United States Government Printing Office, 1968. Pp. 1-67.

CARR, EDWARD HALLETT. *The Romantic Exiles.* Baltimore: Penguin Books, Inc., 1949.

CLAUSEWITZ, KARL VON. *On War.* Washington, D.C.: The Infantry Journal Press, 1943.

CLEAVER, ELDRIDGE. "A Candid Conversation with the Revolutionary Leader of the Black Panthers," *Playboy,* December 1968, pp. 89-108, 238.

CLOWARD, RICHARD A., and LLOYD E. OHLIN. *Delinquency and Opportunity.* New York: The Free Press, 1960.

COLEMAN, JAMES. S. *Community Conflict.* New York: The Free Press, 1967.

CORVO, FREDERICK BARON. *A History of the Borgias.* New York: Modern Library, Inc., 1931.

COSER, LEWIS A. *Continuities in the Study of Social Conflict.* New York: The Free Press, 1967.

DAHENDORF, RALF. *Class and Class Conflict in Industrial Society.* Stanford, Calif.: Stanford University Press, 1959.

DARROW, CLARENCE. *The Story of My Life.* New York: Grosset & Dunlap, Inc., 1932.

DOLCI, DANILO. *Waste.* New York: Monthly Review Press, 1964.

DOSTOYEVSKY, FYODOR. *The Possessed.* Trans. Constance Garnett. New York: Modern Library, Inc., 1936.

DUBLIN, LOUIS I. *Suicide: A Sociological and Statistical Study.* New York; The Ronald Press Company, 1963.

EASTON, DAVID. *A Systems Analysis of Political Life.* New York: John Wiley & Sons, Inc., 1965.

ECKSTEIN, HARRY, ed. *Internal War: Problems and Approaches.* New York: The Free Press, 1964.

ELLIOT, MABEL A. *Crime in Modern Society.* New York: Harper & Row, Publishers, 1952.

ELLUL, JACQUES. *The Technological Society.* New York: Random House, Inc., 1964.

EMMET, DOROTHY. "The Concept of Power," *Proceedings of the Aristotelian Society,* 54 (1954), 13.

ENDLEMAN, SHALOM, ed. *Violence in the Streets.* Chicago: Quadrangle Books, Inc., 1968.

ETZIONI, AMITAI, and EVA ETZIONI, eds. *Social Change: Sources,*

Patterns, and Consequences. New York: Basic Books, Inc., Publishers, 1964.

FELDMAN, ARNOLD S. "Violence and Volatility: The Likelihood of Revolution" in Eckstein, 1964, pp. 111-29.

FOGELSON, ROBERT M, and ROBERT B. HILL. "Who Riots? A Study of Participation in the 1967 Riots," *Supplemental Studies for the National Advisory Commission on Civil Disorders.* Washington, D.C.: United States Government Printing Office, 1968. pp. 217-45.

FRAZER, JAMES GEORGE. *The Golden Bough: A Study in Magic and Religion.* New York: The Macmillan Company, 1956.

GLASER, DANIEL. "The Sociological Approach to Crime and Correction," *Law and Contemporary Problems,* Autumn 1958, pp. 681-702.

GORER, GEOFFREY. "Man Has No Killer Instinct," in Montagu, 1968, pp. 27-37.

GREGG, RICHARD B. *The Power of Nonviolence.* New York: Schocken Books, 1966.

GRIMSHAW, ALLEN D. "Government and Social Violence." *The Minnesota Review,* III, 2 (Winter, 1963), 236-45.

GROSS, FELIKS. "Politics of Violence: Terror and Political Assassination in Eastern Europe and Russia." Unpublished manuscript, prepared for the National Commission on the Causes and Prevention of Violence, 1968.

GUARESCHI, GIOVANNI. *My Secret Diary, 1943-1945.* Trans. Frances Frenaye. New York: Farrar, Straus & Giroux, Inc., 1951.

GUEVARA, ERNESTO "CHE." *Guerilla Warfare.* Trans. J.P. Morray. New York: Random House, Inc., 1968.

HASLUCK, MARGARET. *The Unwritten Law in Albania.* Ed. J.H. Hutton. Cambridge, England: Cambridge University Press, 1954.

HAVENS, MURRAY C. "Assassination in Australia." Unpublished manuscript, prepared for the National Commission on the Causes and Prevention of Violence, 1968.

HEAPS, WILLARD A. *Riots, U.S.A.: 1765-1965.* New York: The Seabury Press, Inc., 1966.

HENRY, ANDREW F., and JAMES F. SHORT, JR. *Suicide and Homicide: Some Economic, Sociological, and Psychological Aspects of Aggression.* New York: The Free Press, 1954.

HOFFMANN, STANLEY. *The State of War: Essays on the Theory and Practice of International Politics.* New York: Frederick A. Praeger, Inc., 1965.

HOMANS, GEORGE C. *Social Behavior: Its Elementary Forms.* New York: McGraw-Hill Book Company, 1961.

JANOWITZ, MORRIS. *Social Control of Escalated Riots.* Chicago: The University of Chicago Center for Policy Study, 1968.

JOHNSON, CHALMERS. *Revolutionary Change.* Boston: Little, Brown and Company, 1966.

JOHNSON, ELMER HUBERT. *Crime, Correction, and Society.* Homewood, Ill.: Dorsey Press, 1964.

KEFAUVER, ESTES. *Crime in America.* New York: Doubleday & Company, 1951.

KOESTLER, ARTHUR. *The Ghost in the Machine.* New York: The Macmillan Company, 1967.

KOPKIND, ANDREW. "Are We in the Middle of a Revolution?" *New York Times Magazine,* November 10, 1968, pp. 54-59, 64-69.

KRISTOL, IRVING. "The Old Politics, The New Politics, The *New* New Politics," *New York Times Magazine,* November 24, 1968.

LAPIERE, RICHARD T. *Social Change.* New York: McGraw-Hill Book Company, 1965.

―――. *A Theory of Social Control.* New York: McGraw-Hill Book Company, 1954.

LASSWELL, HAROLD D. *The Future of Political Science.* New York: Atherton Press, 1963.

LEIDEN, CARL. "Assassination in the Middle East," unpublished manuscript, 1968.

―――, and KARL M. SCHMITT, eds. *The Politics of Violence: Revolution in the Modern World.* Englewood Cliffs, N.J.: Prentice-Hall, Inc., 1968.

LEIGHTON, JOSEPH A. *Social Philosophers in Conflict.* New York: Appleton-Century-Crofts, 1937.

LEVINE, VICTOR T. "The Course of Political Violence," in William H. Lewis, ed., *French Speaking Africa: The Search for Identity.* New York: Appleton-Century-Crofts, 1965. Pp. 59-68.

LEWIS, BERNARD. *The Assassins: A Radical Sect in Islam.* New York: Basic Books, Inc., Publishers, 1968.

LEWIS, NORMAN. *The Honored Society.* New York: G.P. Putnam's

Sons, 1964.

LINDESMITH, ALFRED, and ANSELM STRAUSS. *Social Psychology.* New York: The Dryden Press, 1949.

MACIVER, R.M. "The Role of the Precipitant," in Etzioni, 1964, pp. 421-26.

———. "The Role of the Precipitating Event," in *Social Causation.* Boston: Ginn and Company, 1942.

———. *The Web of Government.* New York: McGraw-Hill Book Company, 1947.

MCLUHAN, MARSHALL. *Understanding Media: The Extensions of Man.* New York: The New American Library, Inc., 1964.

———. *War and Peace in the Global Village.* New York: McGraw-Hill Book Company, 1968.

MAILER, NORMAN. "Talking of Violence," interviewed by W.J. Weatherby in Endleman, 1968, pp. 85-91.

MANNHEIM, KARL. "Sociology of Knowledge," in *Ideology and Utopia.* New York: Harcourt, Brace & World, Inc., 1936.

MASOTTI, LEWIS. "Violent Protest in Urban Society," paper presented at the 1967 meeting of American Academy for the Advancement of Science, unpublished.

MAZRUI, ALI A. "Thoughts on Assassination in Africa," *Political Science Quarterly,* LXXXIII, 1 (March 1968), 40-52.

MERTON, ROBERT K. *Social Theory and Social Structure.* New York: The Free Press, 1957.

MESSICK, HANK. *The Silent Syndicate.* New York: The Macmillan Company, 1967.

MILLER, ARTHUR. "The Bored and the Violent," in Endleman, 1968, pp. 270-80.

MONTAGU, M.R. ASHLEY, ed. *Man and Aggression.* London: Oxford University Press, 1968.

MOONEY, MARTIN. *Crime Incorporated.* New York: Whittlesey House, 1935.

MORRIS, DESMOND. *The Naked Ape: A Zoologist's Study of the Human Animal.* New York: McGraw-Hill Book Company, 1968.

MUMFORD, LEWIS. *The Myth of the Machine. Technics and Human Development.* New York: Harcourt, Brace, & World, Inc., 1967.

———. *The Urban Prospect.* New York: Harcourt, Brace, & World,

Inc., 1968.

NIEBURG, H.L. "The Uses of Violence," *Journal of Conflict Resolution*, March 1963, pp. 43-55.

OPPENHEIM, FELIX E. *Dimensions of Freedom: An Analysis*. New York: St. Martin's Press, 1961.

ORTEGA Y GASSET, JOSE. *Concord and Liberty*. Trans. Helene Weyl. New York: W.W. Norton & Company, Inc., 1946.

————. *The Revolt of the Masses*. New York: W.W. Norton & Company, Inc., 1932.

PARSONS, TALCOTT. "Some Reflections on the Place of Force in Social Process," in Eckstein, 1964, pp. 33-70.

PETTIGREW, THOMAS F., and ROSALIND B. SPIER. "The Econological Structure of Negro Homicide," *American Journal of Sociology*, LXIV, 6 (May 1962), 621-29.

PYE, LUCIAN W. "The Roots of Insurgency and the Commencement of Rebellions" in Eckstein, 1964, pp. 157-79.

REID, ED. *Mafia*. New York: The New American Library, Inc., 1952, 1964.

RUSSELL, BERTRAND. *Power: A New Social Analysis*. London: Unwin Books, 1962.

SANGER, RICHARD H. *Insurgent Era*. Washington, D.C.: Potomac Books, Inc., 1967.

SCHALLER, GEORGE B. *The Year of the Gorilla*. Chicago: University of Chicago Press, 1964.

SCHELLING, THOMAS C. *Arms and Influence*. New Haven, Conn.: Yale University Press, 1964.

SCHMITT, KARL M. "Assassination in Latin America." Unpublished manuscript, prepared for the National Commission on the Causes and Prevention of Violence, 1968.

SCHMOOKLER, JACOB. *Invention and Economic Growth*. Cambridge, Mass.. Harvard University Press, 1966.

SCHRAMM, MELVIN, JACK LYLE, and EDWIN B. PARKER. *Television in the Lives of Our Children*. Stanford, Calif.: Stanford University Press, 1961. Pp. 237-38.

SCHULTZ, DUANE P. *Panic Behavior: Discussion and Readings*. New York: Random House, Inc., 1964.

SCHULTZ, L.G. "Why the Negro Carries Weapons," *Journal of Criminal Law, Criminology and Political Science*, LIII, 4 (1962),

476-83.

SERVICE, ELMAN R. *Primitive Social Organization: An Evolutionary Perspective.* New York: Random House, Inc., 1962.

SHAW, GEORGE BERNARD. "The Revolutionist's Handbook," in *Man and Superman.* Cambridge, Mass.: The University Press, 1903. Pp. 177-224.

SHIBUTANI, TAMOTSU. "Reference Groups as Perspective," *American Journal of Sociology,* LX, 3 (May 1955), 559-68.

SIMMEL, GEORG. *Conflict and the Web of Group Affiliations.* New York: The Free Press, 1955.

SIMON, RITA JAMES. "Political Violence Directed at Public Office Holders: A Brief Analysis of the American Scene." Unpublished manuscript, prepared for the National Commission on the Causes and Prevention of Violence, 1968.

SNYDER, GLENN H. *Deterrence and Defense: Toward a Theory of National Security.* Princeton, N.J.: Princeton University Press, 1961.

SOREL, GEORGES. *Reflections on Violence.* Paris, 1905. New York: The Macmillan Company, 1961.

SOUKUP, JAMES R. "Assassination in Japan." Unpublished manuscript; prepared for the National Commission on the Causes and Prevention of Violence, 1968.

STANTON, ALFRED H., and STEWARD E. PERCY, eds. *Personality and Political Crisis.* New York: The Free Press, 1951.

SUMNER, WILLIAM GRAHAM. *Folkways: A Study of the Sociological Importance of Usages, Manners, Customs, Mores, and Morals.* New York: The New American Library, Inc., 1940.

TARDE, GABRIEL. *Penal Philosophy.* Trans. R. Howell. Boston: Little, Brown and Company, 1912.

THOMPSON, CRAIG, and ALLEN RAYMOND. *Gang Rule in New York: The Story of a Lawless Era.* New York: The Dial Press, Inc., 1960.

THORNTON, THOMAS PERRY. "Terror as a Weapon of Political Agitation," in Eckstein, 1964, pp. 71-99.

TILLICH, PAUL. *Love, Power, and Justice.* New York: Oxford University Press, 1961.

TOMLINSON, T.M. "Negro Reaction to the Los Angeles Riot and the Development of a Riot Ideology." Unpublished manuscript, prepared for the National Commission on the Causes and Prevention of Violence, 1968.

TRETIAK, DAVID. "Reflections on Political Assassinations in China." Unpublished manuscript, prepared for the National Commission on the Causes and Prevention of Violence, 1968.

TURKUS, BURTON B., and SID FEDER. *Murder, Inc.: The Story of "The Syndicate."* New York: Farrar, Straus & Giroux, Inc., 1951.

UNITED STATES CONGRESS, SENATE COMMITTEE ON GOVERNMENT OPERATIONS, SUBCOMMITTEE ON INVESTIGATIONS. *Hearings on Organized Crime and Illicit Traffic in Narcotics,* Parts I and II. September-October 1963. 88th Congress, 1st Session. Washington: United States Government Printing Office, 1963.

UNITED STATES CONGRESS, SENATE SPECIAL COMMITTEE TO INVESTIGATE ORGANIZED CRIME IN INTERSTATE COMMERCE. *Third Interim Report Pursuant to S. Res. 202. A Resolution to Investigate Gambling and Racketeering Activities.* Report No. 307. 82nd Congress, 1st. Session, 1951. New York: Arco Publishing Co., Inc., 1951.

WALTER, E.V. "Power and Violence," *American Political Science Review,* XXIX, 3 (June 1964), 350-55.

WARSHOW, ROBERT. *The Immediate Experience.* New York: Doubleday & Company, Inc., 1962.

WEBER, MAX. *The Theory of Social and Economic Organization.* Trans. A.M. Henderson and Talcott Parsons. New York: The Free Press, 1947.

WOLFGANG, MARVIN E. *Patterns in Criminal Homicide.* Philadelphia: University of Pennsylvania, 1958.

YABLONSKY, LEWIS. "The New Criminal: A Report on the 'Hip' Killer," *Saturday Review,* February 2, 1963.

INDEX

Abrahamsen, David, 136
Albanian peasants, reintegration among, 92
Alinsky, Saul, 151
Ambivalence in social life, 55
American Indians, 148
American revolution, use of word-of-mouth communication during, 31
Anomic behavior-elitist behavior, 121
Ardrey, Robert, Social Darwinism in writings of, 36, 37
Ardrey-Lorenz view: of man as his own worst enemy, 37; ethological evidence against, 39
Arendt, Hannah, 54, 55, 146
Armaments race, role of in international conflict, 23
Assassin: the mind of, 6, 7; in relation to social process, 15
Assassination: as a commonplace political tactic, 9, 14; as a possible outcome of social dynamics, 16; by the Mafia, 116-117; relation to death-wish, 122-123; legitimization of series, 146; of student leaders in Latin America, 157; impossibility of eliminating, 159
Auden, W. H., 46, 52
Australia, violence in pioneer history of, 24
Authority: relationships and bargaining, 50; hierarchies of, 57, 94, 95, 105; as issue behind disputes, 60; authority issues v. policy issues, 111

Backlash: in analytical models of social reform, 42; effect on behavior, 81; effect on black militants, 148; of S. I. Hayakawa, 158
Bantu tribes, reintegration among, 92